South Florida's CELEBRITY CHEFS

Sponsored by
THE MONTEREY VINEYARD

Proceeds to benefit the
MUSEUM OF ART
Fort Lauderdale

Compiled by the Contemporaries

Foreword by DON SHULA

PEANUT BUTTER PUBLISHING
SEATTLE, WASHINGTON

First Printing—September, 1987
10 9 8 7 6 5 4 3 2

Peanut Butter Publishing
329-2nd Avenue W.
Seattle, WA 98119

206-281-5965

ISBN #0-89716-201-3

CONTENTS

MIAMI DOLPHINS

MIAMI DOLPHINS, LTD
4770 BISCAYNE BLVD., SUITE 1440
MIAMI, FLORIDA 33137
(305) 576-1000

JOSEPH ROBBIE
Managing General Partner

It takes more to make a winning team than just winning games. It takes a commitment from each player to give his best for the good of the team and the community that supports it. The Miami Dolphins have made that commitment to South Florida.

There are other "teams" that have also made commitments to South Florida.

<u>South Florida Celebrity Chefs</u> is the result of the Contemporaries' team commitment to support the Museum of Art in Fort Lauderdale and culture in our community.

As it takes many players to make up a great football team, it takes all of us to support the arts and the many other advantages that make South Florida a great place to live.

It is my pleasure to write this introduction for <u>South Florida Celebrity Chefs</u> and to be a part of another winning team.

Don Shula

THE
MONTEREY VINEYARD®

CARY GOTT
Executive Vice President
Winemaster

Since I am a winemaker, you won't be surprised to learn
that I think winemaking is an art. Once in a while I get
the time to consider other forms of art....and that has
been a pleasure in my visits to Ft. Lauderdale.

Stone Crabs! Posh Squash! Schizophrenic Tuna! Mayoralty
Headache Stew! Mayonnaise Kisses! The recipes ahead are a
treasure trove of sensory experiences, and we are thrilled
that the Museum of Art will become part of that experience
for you.

Enjoy your meanderings through the worlds of culture and
cuisine, and come visit us if your senses find you in
Monterey County, California!

Cary Gott

800 SOUTH ALTA STREET • POST OFFICE BOX 780-GONZALES, CALIFORNIA 93926 • (408) 675-2481

MUSEUM OF ART

July 10, 1987

Dear Friend of the Museum of Art, Fort Lauderdale and Fellow Gourmet:

Thank the "Contemporaries", a wonderful group of young people (40 years old is their limit) for this outstanding book of recipes or should I say "sins". Fernando Botero must be their Artist Laureate.

Our Museum, shiny and new, presents South Florida's foremost art exhibitions. The members of the Museum have, for 29 years, strived to bring Fort Lauderdale an increasingly erudite and artful year-round program that piques the interest of our entire community from school children to scholars and from the "Red Barn with the Green Tree" school to the derivatives of Bau-haus such as the Modern Constructivist Movement.

Although the Museum has not confined the scope of its collections or programs to a narrow focus, we do concentrate on International Modern Art from the 19th and 20th Centuries, both figurative and abstract.

Foremost among our collection is the Meyer & Golda Marks gift of some 200 hundred paintings, 50 sculptures and 2000 prints from the CoBrA School, making our museum the foremost place in the United States for these works of art.

The Museum will aim to exhibit contemporary artists, so we collectors can enjoy broadening our own expertise in the art we can afford to collect. We will also do a few major shows, bringing to South Florida the works of major artists. Our superb Director, Mr. George Bolge, each year produces an outstanding exhibition schedule.

On behalf of our former Presidents:

James B. Kerr (the founding President & President Emeritus)	1960-1961
William J. Godfrey	1962-1963
Thor Amlie	1963-1964
R. M. Gardner (our continuing General Counsel)	1964-1967
Herbert Jenne	1967-1968
John F. Coulton	1968-1969
Mrs. Francis T. McCahill (our Chairman Emeritus - the soul of our growth)	1969-1975
Elliott Barnett (the great builder of dreams)	1975-1987

and on behalf of some of our other generous benefactors,
Mr. and Mrs. Henry Hope, August Urbanek, Maurice Lipschultz,
Robert Williamson, Mr. and Mrs. Walter Griffith, Mr. and Mrs.
Donald Ozmun and many others, and from all the Museum
members, we have but one aim:

> "To gather together Florida's Art Lovers,
> Artists and Collectors in a membership
> - really a club - dedicated to fine art
> and the cherished happiness it brings
> to the family of man."

Sincerely yours,

Michael S. Egan
President

MSE:bm

STEVEN CLIPPINGER

museum of art

CONTEMPORARIES

   You may not be stopped by admiring fans in the supermarket, but
you'll surely receive rave reviews at home by using this new cookbook
sponsored by the Museum of Art Contemporaries. What better way to gain
celebrity status than by serving dishes that have inspired and nourished
the notables who have helped put South Florida on the map.

   By using this cookbook, you will be contributing to the continued
success of Fort Lauderdale's own stellar attraction, our Museum of Art.
Funds raised through cookbook sales will be used to support the museum's
exhibitions and educational programs and the development of its outstanding
permanent collection.

   The Contemporaries would especially like to thank Laura Sayles who
has chaired this project and Cary Gott of The Monterey Vineyard and The
Seagram Classics Wine Company for allowing us to be the sponsoring organi-
zation. It is by the generosity of The Monterey Vineyard through their
funding, direction, publication and marketing efforts that this book was
made possible.

   We hope you will enjoy this cookbook and that it may inspire you to
develop your culinary skills toward a higher art.

Sincerely,

Rob Rose, President
Museum of Art Contemporaries

ACKNOWLEDGEMENTS

To all the celebrities who shared their favorite culinary triumphs, a special thanks.

Many thanks to the cookbook committee whose work was invaluable: Diane Balogh, Chris Feeley, Pamela Gilman, Tim Kimes, William R. Leonard, Cindy Lotz, Deborah Needham, Carol Reichbaum, Rob Rose, President of the Contemporaries; Laura Sayles, Chairwoman; Patricia Schmitt, Leni Smith, Alicia Wattley, and Kathy Webster. To all the Contemporaries whose support has been unwavering, thank you.

The general membership of the Museum of Art, and its director George Bolge; the Board of Trustees, especially Jeannine Marrinson.

Cary Gott of The Monterey Vineyard.

Dilly Hackleman and Martha Burgess for cover design.

The Museum of Art Contemporaries wishes to thank Samuel Bronfman, II, President of Seagram Classics Wine Co., for his extreme generosity and help without which this project would not have become a reality.

THE BREAKERS

CHICKEN CARMEL

Serves 4 Persons

4   4-Ounce Chicken Breasts, Boned
6   Ounces Crab (Body Meat)
1   Teaspoon Chopped Shallots
1   Cup Sliced, Fresh Mushrooms
1   Tablespoon Chopped Fresh Chives
1   Tablespoon Chopped Pimientos
1   Egg
Sliced Raw Almonds, Chopped
Flour for Dredging
Egg Wash
½ Cup Butter, Clarified

Sauce

2   Tablespoons Butter & 2 Tablespoons Flour (for roux)
1½ Cups Chicken Stock
½   Cup White Wine
Salt & Pepper (White) to Taste
Worchestershire Sauce to Taste

In two to three tablespoons of clarified butter, brown shallots with mushrooms until mushrooms exude juices and the liquid is reduced, add chives and pimientos. Mix, fold in crab meat and egg, reserving 1 teaspoon to set aside.

Flatten chicken breasts, skin side down. Divide crab meat mixture into 4 equal portions and place on chicken breasts. Roll. Before going to the next step, place stuffed breast in freezer for a few minutes to slightly firm.

Lightly dust firm stuffed breast with flour, dip in egg wash, then in almonds. Lightly brown in skillet with remaining clarified butter to seal flavors. Then place in lightly buttered pan, seam side down, and cover with foil. Bake in a 325 degree oven, for 25 minutes or until done.

To make the sauce: Mix melted butter and flour over low heat. Stirring continuously, cook a few minutes until you notice a slight color change. Continuing to stir, slowly add chicken stock, bring it to a simmer. Next add wine, bring to a boiling point and simmer until thickened.

This entree is very attractive when served. To serve, cut in slices crosswise - stuffing showing. Serve the sauce on each plate and place chicken roll over the sauce. Serve additional sauce on the side.

Clayton Addison
President

BENIHANA NATIONAL CORP.

ROCKY H. AOKI
CHAIRMAN OF THE BOARD

Dear Adventurous Diner:

In 1964 when I opened my first Benihana restaurant it was important to let people know that while we had a Japanese name and theme, we really served all American steaks, chicken and shrimp. One of the things we capitalized on was the fact that we did, however, bring along certain age-old recipes from my native country. My favorite, which is a ginger salad dressing that dates back more than 1,000 years, first appeared on our menu after our chief chef made his special modifications making it more appealing to the American palate.

THE BENIHANA SUPERB SALAD DRESSING

1/4	cup sliced celery
1/4	cup soybean oil
2	tablespoons coarsely chopped onion
2	tablespoons white vinegar
1	tablespoon tomato paste
1-1½	teaspoons soy sauce
1/4	teaspoon each salt and ground ginger

Combine all ingredients in blender container or work bowl of food processor fitted with steel knife; process until almost smooth. Makes 6 servings, about 2 tablespoons each (unused portions may be stored in a covered container in the refrigerator).

Ita Da Ki Masu (Bon Apetit),

Rocky H. Aoki
Chairman

8685 N. W. 53rd Terrace, Miami, Florida 33166

Agnes Ash
PUBLISHER

SUGARY APPLE MUFFINS
2 1/4 cups all-purpose flour
1/2 cup sugar
3 1/2 teaspoons baking powder
1/2 teaspoon salt
1/2 teaspoon cinnamon
2 eggs
4 tablespoons shortening (melted)
1 cup milk
1 cup apples chopped fine

TOPPING
2 tablespoons sugar
1 teaspoon cinnamon
1 teaspoon nutmeg

1. Sift dry ingredients. 2. Add eggs, shortening and milk which have been combined. 3. Mix lightly until dry ingredients are moistened. Add apples. 4. Fill greased muffin tins 2/3 full. 5. Sprinkle topping on each muffin. 6. Bake at 400 degrees for 25 minutes. Makes about one dozen muffins.

Agnes Ash

LAW OFFICES

GREENBERG, TRAURIG, ASKEW, HOFFMAN, LIPOFF, ROSEN & QUENTEL, P.A.

III NORTH ORANGE AVENUE • SUITE 1550
ORLANDO, FLORIDA 32801
TELEPHONE (305) 841-2222
TELECOPIER (305) 422-2766

MIAMI OFFICE
BRICKELL CONCOURS
1401 BRICKELL AVENUE
MIAMI, FLORIDA 33131
(305) 579-0500

WEST PALM BEACH OFFICE
100 AUSTRALIAN AVENUE
SUITE 201
WEST PALM BEACH, FLORIDA 33406
(305) 683-6611
TELECOPIER (305) 683-8447

BROWARD OFFICE
110 EAST BROWARD BOULEVARD
SUITE 1650
FORT LAUDERDALE, FLORIDA 33301
(305) 765-0500

REUBIN O'D. ASKEW
841-2222

PLEASE REPLY TO:
ORLANDO OFFICE

Donna Lou Askew's Recipe for:

APPLE WALNUT SQUARES

4 CUPS COARSELY CHOPPED, PEELED APPLES
2 CUPS SUGAR
2 EGGS, SLIGHTLY BEATEN
1/2 CUP VEGETABLE OIL
2 CUPS FLOUR
2 TEASPOONS BAKING SODA
2 TEASPOONS CINNAMON
1/2 TEASPOON SALT
1 CUP BLACK WALNUT PIECES

Combine apples and sugar and let stand until sugar is absorbed and moist, about 45 minutes. Beat eggs and vegetable oil together by hand. Sift flour, baking soda, cinnamon and salt together. Stir alternately with apple-sugar mixture. Stir in black walnut pieces.

Bake in greased, floured 13 by 9 by 2 inch pan in 350° oven for one hour. Orange or lemon butter frosting is optional.

We enjoy serving it warm with whipped cream or ice cream. We frequently served it at Mansion events in Tallahassee and it was enjoyed by the men as well as the ladies.

Reubin O'D. Askew

4

Elaine Azen

TEX MEX BRUNCH BAKE

1 1/4 lb. Summer squash or zucchini
4 eggs
1/2 Cup Milk
1 lb. Jack cheese (cubed)
1 tsp. Salt (optional)
1 tsp. Baking Powder
1/4 Cup Chopped Parsley
1/2 tsp. Fine Herbes
1 Cup Roasted and peeled green pepper (Ortega chili)
1/2 Cup Kellogg's Corn Flakes crumbs
1/4 Cup Butter or Margarine

Cook squash (sliced) until almost tender. Drain well, mix all ingredients with squash which has been cooked (except butter and crumbs). Butter casserole dish and sprinkle with part of crumbs. Add squash mixture with remaining crumbs. Dot with remainder of butter.

Bake 30 minutes in 350 degree oven - uncovered.

PEPPY, SPICEY AND DELICIOUS!!

Enjoy...

Elaine

Since I am primarily a vegetarian and can eat very limited amounts of protein, my own recipes deal principally with vegetables. This is a great one taking into account two of my favorite vegetables, artichokes and carrots. I recommend it as a first course, and it will serve two people.

Artichoke Bottoms Filled with Herbed Carrots

2 artichokes, trimmed into bottoms (procedure follows)
2 tablespoons olive oil
¼ cup dry white wine
1½ cups canned chicken broth
1 teaspoon fresh lemon juice
½ teaspoon dried oregano, crumbled
½ teaspoon dried marjoram, crumbled
½ teaspoon dried thyme, crumbled
½ cup thinly sliced carrots
1 tablespoon minced fresh parsley leaves

With a spoon scrape the chokes from the artichoke bottoms and return the artichoke bottoms to some acidulated water (water with ½ lemon juice). In a saucepan combine the oil, the wine, the broth, the juice from ½ lemon, the oregano, the marjoram, the thyme, and salt and pepper to taste and bring the liquid to a boil. Add the artichokes, drained, and simmer for 15 minutes. Add the carrots and simmer the vegetables for 5 to 10 minutes, or until the artichokes are tender. Transfer the artichokes concave side up to serving plates and mound half the carrots in each bottom. Spoon the cooking liquid over the artichokes and sprinkle the carrots with the parsley.

FROM THE
DESK OF ....

CECIL BEACH

BRUNSWICK STEW

1 4 lb.stewing chicken (cut up)
2 qts. water
2 tsp. salt
½ cup catsup
2 tsp. Worchestershire sauce
½ tsp. hot pepper sauce
3 tbs. butter or margarine
grated rind & juice of ½ lemon
2 1 lb.cans tomatoes (or 8 fresh)
4 med. potatoes, diced
4 cups baby lima beans
4 cups whole kernel corn
2 cups fresh okra cut in ½ inch slices
4 stks celery, cut into ½ inch slices
4 clvs garlic, minced
2 med. onions, minced
salt and pepper to taste

Combine chicken, water and 2 teaspoons salt in large
kettle. Simmer, covered, until meat is tender (3-4
hours.) Remove chicken and cool. Remove skin and
then meat from bones. Cut meat into bite size pieces.
Skim the cooking stock and return pieces of meat
to kettle. Add remaining ingredients, simmer, stirring
occasionally until mixture is thick, about 2 hours.
Serves 8.

SUNBEAM TELEVISION CORPORATION

KEY LIME PIE   JILL BEACH, ANCHOR/REPORTER
_____

INGREDIENTS:

4 EGGS (SEPARATE YOLKS FROM WHITES)
1 CAN BORDEN'S MAGNOLIA SWEETENED CONDENSED MILK
1/8 TSP. OF SALT
4 OZ. (OR JUICE OF 6 TO 7 KEY LIMES)
4 TSPS. SUGAR
1 TSP. VANILLA
1 TSP. KNOX GELATIN (UNFLAVORED)

BEAT THE EGG YOLKS LIGHTLY, ADD SALT AND MILK AND BEAT
UNTIL SMOOTH. DISSOLVE THE GELATIN IN THE LIME JUICE AND
ADD SLOWLY WHILE STIRRING TO THE YOLK AND MILK MIXTURE.
THEN SET ASIDE TO THICKEN.
WHIP THE EGG WHITES WHILE SLOWLY ADDING THE SUGAR AND THEN THE
VANILLA, AND WHIPPING UNTIL THE WHITES PEAK WHEN A KNIFE IS
DRAWN UP OUT OF THEM.
ADD THE WHITES TO THE EGG, MILK AND JUICE MIXTURE BY GENTLY
FOLDING THEM IN AND POUR INTO A PREBAKED OR GRAHAM CRACKER
CRUST 9 INCH PIE .   CHILL FOR SEVERAL HOURS BEFORE SERVING.

YUM! YUM!

THIS IS A LONG-TIME FAMILY RECIPE, WE LOVE IT!

Jill Beach

WSVN/NBC 1401 79th Street Causeway, Miami, Florida 33141 (305) 751-6692

BEBER SILVERSTEIN & PARTNERS

5561 SW Third Avenue / Miami, Florida 55145 / (505) 856-9800

SOUFFLE CHOCOLATE CAKE

Butter

Flour

10 oz. semisweet chocolate, broken into small pieces (Tobler, Maillard, Poullain)

1/2 cup unsalted butter, cut into 8 pieces

6 large eggs, separated

1 cup granulated sugar

1 tb. Grand Marnier

1/2 tsp. vanilla

1 ½ cups heavy cream

3 tb. confectioners sugar

Place oven rack in lower third of oven: heat oven to 375°. Butter and flour bottom and sides of a 9" springform pan.

Melt chocolate with butter in the top of a double boiler. Beat egg yolks in an electric mixer, gradually adding 3/4 cup of the sugar. Beat until yolk mixture is pale yellow and thick, 4 to 6 minutes. Add the chocolate mixture to the yolk mixture, beat until smooth. Add Grand Marnier and vanilla and beat until blended.

Beat the egg whites at high speed until soft peaks form. Gradually beat remaining 1/4 cup of sugar into the whites; continue beating until stiff peaks form. Fold whites gently but thoroughly into chocolate mixture. Pour batter evenly into reserved pan smooth top. Bake 15 minutes at 375°. Reduce temperature to 350° and bake another 15 minutes. Reduce oven temperature to 250° and bake 30 minutes longer. (Total baking time 1 hour). Turn off oven, prop open oven door and allow cake to remain in the oven for 30 minutes. Remove cake from oven and cover top with damp paper toweling; let stand 5 minutes. Remove toweling and cool cake completely. Dome of cake will crack and collapse; this is normal. Press top of cake down lightly to smooth top. Remove springform and transfer cake to serving platter.

Whip cream in chilled mixer bowl until soft peaks form. Add 1 ½ tb. confectioners sugar and beat until a bit stiffer. Dust top of cake with remaining powdered sugar just before serving. Serve cake at room temperature with whipped cream on the side.

Joyce Beber
President

Beber Silverstein & Partners Advertising, Inc. / 542 Madison Avenue / Penthouse / New York, New York 10175 / (212) 985-6440

Diana M Bell
241 Banyan Road
Palm Beach, Florida 33480

I have had many wonderful cooking experiences with Pierre Frany the author of many cook books as well as the "60 Minute Gourmet" column in the New York Times. Whenever Pierre is in Palm Beach or Cohasset Massachusetts we manage to create a delightful feast. One of my favorite recipes is "Duck Salad", shown below. Pierre also helped me when my husband Lowry Bell Jr and I entertained the Queen of Thailand and twenty five of her entourage at lunch in our home in Cohasset with only 24 hours notice. Pierre suggested "Lobster Salad " with a special Mayonnaise he makes from scratch.

Diana's Duck Salad

2- 4 to 5 lb ducklings	2 lbs string beans
4 unblemished sweet red peppers	20 lychee nuts (canned or fresh)
20 small ripe cherry tomatoes	2 mangos(when not available, papaya)
1 medium red Italian onion finely chopped	1 cup macadamia nuts
4 tablespoons chopped fresh coriander	5 tablespoons raspberry vinegar
1/2 cup walnut oil	

Remove excess fat from duckling. Roast in a 450-degree , preheated oven for 1 1/2 hours. This can be done the day before. Wrap the ducks well and refrigerate. Cut meat from the ducks. Discard skin and bones, Cut into neat bite -sized portions. You should have about 4 cups. Set aside. Trim off ends of beans and string if necessary. Cut beans into 2-inch lengths and drop into saucepan of boiling water. Simmer about 5 minutes. Rinse under cold water and drain. Set aside. Core and seed peppers. Cut into lengthwise shreds. Put shreds into boiling water to blanch for about 1 minute only. Run under cold water and drain.

Cut cherry tomatoes in half and set aside. Cut lychee nuts into quarters. Cut mango or papaya into thin strips. Combine oil, vinegar, coriander, onions, and duck meat and toss well. Add remaining ingredients and toss and add salt and pepper to taste. Serve at room temperature to about 12.

Diana M. Bell

SPINACH CREPES

RECIPE FOR FOUR PERSONS

INGREDIENTS

CREPES

24	large spinach leaves
6	large tomatoes seeded and diced
2	oz. olive oil
1	small onion chopped
1	clove garlic
2	artichoke bottoms (preferably fresh) diced small
1	spicy fresh tyme (optional)
	Salt and pepper to taste

METHOD

Sauteed onions and garlic in olive oil for one minute, add
fresh diced tomatoes and tyme, cook for 10-15 minutes until
most of the water is evaporated. Add salt and pepper and
the diced artichoke bottoms.
In salt boiling water blanch spinach leaves for 30 second,
remove into water lay 3 leaves overlaping each other to
form a crepe, fill center of crepes with tomato mixture and
fold into small log (please be sure that the spinach cover
the tomato mixture on all sides).

Jacques H. Benoit
Executive Chef
Mayfair House Hotel.

WPLG/TV10
A POST-NEWSWEEK STATION

My favorite recipe for Chocolate Chip Cookies is as follows:

1 cup white sugar
½ cup brown sugar
½ cup butter
½ cup shortening
1 egg

Combine:

2 cups flour
1 tsp. cream of tartar
2 tsp. soda
½ tsp. salt
1 tsp. vanilla
2 cups Sathers Chocolate Chips

Cream butter, shortening, brown and white sugar.
Add egg and beat.
Add the combined flour, soda, cream of tartar, salt, vanilla and stir.
Stir in chocolate chips.

Drop by teaspoonfuls onto greased cookie sheet.

Bake for 8-10 minutes in 325° oven.

Ann Bishop

WPLG/TV 10 BROADCAST HOUSE 3900 BISCAYNE BOULEVARD MIAMI FLORIDA 33137 • (305) 576-1010
BROWARD NEWS BUREAU 1 FINANCIAL PLAZA FT. LAUDERDALE FLORIDA 33301 • (305) 763-4577

Gary Bitner Public Relations, Inc.

City Park Place • 1330-B Southeast Fourth Avenue • Fort Lauderdale, Florida 33316 • 305/522-0022 • Miami 305/945-7193
Orlando Office: 999 Woodcock Road • Suite 305 • Orlando, Florida 32803 • 305/898-0993

GARY BITNER'S NEW "RIVER" POTATOES

Ingredients:

1 lb. New potatoes

2 pts. Sour cream

2 jars Caviar

Wash and boil new potatoes (with skins) until they
are soft in the center. (Test with a fork.)
Slice each in half and arrange on tray(s), with the
skin side down. Let cool. Drop a spoonful of
sour cream on the center of each potato half.
(A pastry tube may be used.)
Top with caviar and serve.

Racal-Milgo

1601 N. Harrison Parkway, Sunrise, Florida 33323-2899 Telephone (305) 475-1601

Edward Bleckner, Jr.
Chairman of the Board and
Chief Executive Officer

Zucchini Frittata

4 eggs or 1/2 cup egg whites

Salt and pepper to taste

1/4 cup freshly grated Parmesan cheese

2 tablespoons unsalted margarine or olive oil

1 medium onion, thinly sliced

2 zucchini, thinly sliced

2 tablespoons chopped parsley

2 teaspoons minced garlic

Melt margarine in 12" non stick skillet. Add onion and saute over medium heat for 1 minute. Add zucchini, parsley and garlic, saute 4 minutes or until lightly browned. Beat eggs or whites lightly with salt, pepper and Parmesan. Remove zucchini mixture with a slotted spoon and stir into egg mixture. Add more margarine to skillet if necessary. Add egg mixture and cook over medium heat 5 minutes. Place plate on top of the skillet and turn frittata onto plate. Slide the frittata back into the skillet, and cook 5 minutes more. Cut in half and serve. Serve two.

Edward Bleckner, Jr.

RACAL

Kim's Easy Chicken Cacciatore

4-6 Boneless Chicken Breasts - Remove Fat

1 Large Jar or Can Marinara Sauce

1. Med. Red Bell Pepper - Sliced in Thin Strips

1 Med. Green Bell Pepper - Sliced in Thin Strips

1 Onion Sliced or Chopped - Not too fine

2-3 Cups Fresh Mushrooms Sliced

2 Cloves Garlic Minced

2 Tsp. Oregano - or more - ?

A pinch or 2 of Sweet Basil

Salt & Pepper

In Casserole Dish put a coating of sauce on the bottom. Place pieces of Red and Green Peppers, Onion, mushroom and a little garlic on sauce. Lay chicken pieces on top of veggies, being careful not to overlap. Add drops of sauce. Put garlic, oregano, Basil, salt and pepper on next. Put remaining veggies on next then cover with remaining sauce.

Place in preheated oven, about 350° for about 25-30 min. or until chicken is cooked white.

Serve over Linguine noodles

Kim Bohanan

15

MUSEUM OF ART

GEORGE S. BOLGE, EXECUTIVE DIRECTOR

CHICKEN CAMPAGNE

(Serves 6-8)

1 Five Pound Chicken or 2 Two and a Half Pound Chickens, disjointed
3/4 cup flour
2 teaspoons salt
freshly ground pepper
1 teaspoon thyme

3 – 4 cloves garlic, minced
1/2 cup celery, coarsely chopped
1 bunch green onions, bottoms diced
1/4 cup fresh parsley, coarsely chopped
2 – 3 medium carrots, julienned
3 medium turnips, peeled and cut into sixths or eighths
1 pound mushrooms, halved or sliced
1½ cups chicken stock
3/4 cup dry white wine
2-3 bay leaves
1/2 teaspoon dried rosemary or 2 sprigs fresh rosemary
freshly ground pepper to taste

Combine flour, salt, pepper and thyme in brown paper bag. Place chicken pieces, one or two at a time, in bag and shake until well coated. Brown chicken in heavy skillet. Remove from skillet and place on paper towels to absorb oil. Saute celery, green onions and parsley, adding garlic for last few minutes of cooking. Remove and set aside.

Assemble chicken, carrots, turnips, and mushrooms in large casserole. Add celery, onions, parsley and garlic, chicken stock, wine, bay leaves, rosemary, and pepper.

Bake in preheated 350° oven for 50-60 minutes or until turnips and chicken are done. Serve on bed of rice.

George S. Bolge
Executive Director
Museum of Art

16

ONE EAST LAS OLAS BOULEVARD, FORT LAUDERDALE, FLORIDA 33301-1807. 305/525-5500

Cereche en tortilla   serves 8

1 lb red snapper
3 fresh jalapeño peppers
1 large ripe tomatoe
1 onion
1 bunch cilantro
6 limes
8 corn tortillas
Oil for frying

Cut the red snapper, jalapeño peppers, tomatoe, and onion into bite size pieces. Chop the cilantro. Mix the above ingredients with the juice of the limes. Marinate overnight in the refridgerator. Before serving, deep fry the tortillas in oil, until crisp and golden brown. Top each tortilla with a portion of the cereche. Garnish with a sprig of cilantro and serve imediately.

Enjoy!!

Jillian Bos

3734 Justison Road
Coconut Grove, Florida 33133

I'm a native Miamian and have always enjoyed the great fresh
delicacies from the sea that are so abundant here in South Florida,
Here is a quick and delicious recipe for fish.

INGREDIENTS:

About 4 fish fillets (grouper, yellowtail, kingfish, etc.)
2 tbs. butter or margarine melted
1 cup white wine
1/2 cup lemon juice
bunch of chopped parsley
1 tsp. chopped shallots
1/2 cup cream
salt and pepper to taste
2 cups fresh spinach

Brush the fish with the melted butter and add salt and pepper.
Put on cookie sheet with sides,or baking pan.
Pour half the wine and half the lemon juice over fish
bake at 350 for about 15 minutes (till fish flakes)

Make the sauce by putting parsley, spinach and shallots in a pan
to saute for about 5 minutes, add the rest of wine and lemon juice
and keep cooking, take some fish stock (about 1 cup add to saute
mixture and put all in blender with cream and blend well.

This is the sauce for you to pour over baked fish.

A baked potato and a mixed green salad and you have a
delicious healthy meal.

Enjoy!

Irene Richard Brandon

Gilmore Broadcasting Corporation

MIAMI DOLPHINS

MIAMI DOLPHINS, LTD.
4770 BISCAYNE BLVD., SUITE 1440
MIAMI, FLORIDA 33137
(305) 576-1000

JOSEPH ROBBIE
Managing General Partner

Chicken Fajita Dinner   serves 6-8

3-4 lbs. boneless chicken breasts
large green pepper
large red pepper
1 medium purple onion
1 medium yellow onion

3 large tomatoes
Italian Dressing

Chop all ingrediants and marinade in dressing at least 4 hrs.
Heat skillet and cook fajitas until chicken is completely white
Serve in tortilla - wrap like a burrito - may add guacamole, sour cream and/or salsa

Beans -
Place 1 large can Old El Paso refried beans in pan on stove and add as much milk to make them as creamy as you would like - heat on low to medium

Rice -
Fry 1 small onion and 1½ cup white rice in butter until rice is brown - add 1 can chicken broth, 1 can water and 2 tomatoes chopped to rice - cover and steam until liquid has disappeared

Serve with Coronas and Margaritas!
Muey Bueno!

Bob Brudzinski
#59

19

WPLG/TV10
A POST·NEWSWEEK STATION

DATE   today

TO   my favorite Channel 10 viewers

FROM   Greg Budell

RE   "EYEWITNESS HOT FUDGE"

Thanks for writing! Here's the recipe!

YOU WILL NEED-   5 Squares Bakers Unsweetened chocolate
1¼ cups sugar
1 cup evaporated milk
1 stick of butter (Not margarine!)
1 dash of vanilla extract

READY? Combine the evaporated milk and sugar in a saucepan and bring to
a boil over high heat, stirring the entire time. At boiling, the mixture
should be foaming beautifully. Take the pan off the stove and let it sit
for one minute. This is when you can wrestle your cat.
Put all five squares in the pan and stir them in until they dissolve. Completely.
Stick the butter in and stir that until it dissolves completely/ (sorry- no
whiteout). The mixture should have a nice dark shiny appearance. Stir in
the dash of vanilla and it should still be just warm enough to pour
over ice cream. If you have a problem with this recipe, call me at channel 10.
Everyone I have served this to loves it. The most. And I love you. Thanks!

FAVORITE FISH SANDWICH

Take a fried fish sandwich.
Smother it with cheddar cheese.
Top with fried tomatoes and green Mexican
    chiles.
                    -ALL THE WAY-

"If the phone doesn't ring, it's me."
          —Jimmy Buffett—

MARTA'S PAELLA

Robert E. Butterworth

Serves 10 (Marta cooks generously)

Ingredients

2 pounds shrimp shelled and deveined (leave tails)

1 pound fish (grouper, snapper or scrod)

2 dozen clams (little necks)

2 dozen mussels

6 Florida lobster tails cut into 1 1/2 inch rings with shell
 (or if Maine lobster, shell the tail meat and use claws with
  the shell)

20 stone crab claws

~~2 spanish sausages (chorizo) cut into small rings~~

1/2 pound diced ham

1/2 pound diced pork

1/2 pound chicken pieces

1 pound can of peas

1 pound can tomatoes or tomato sauce

1 1/2 green peppers diced

1 large onion diced

6 garlic cloves crushed

1 8 oz. can pimientos chopped

1 16 oz. can asparagus spears

3 1/2 pounds rice

dash of valencia, preferably (or arborio)

1 teaspoon cumin

2 bay leaves

1/8 teaspoon red pepper

Healthy pinch of saffron

1 teaspoon oregano

2 tablespoons olive oil

1/8 teaspoon bijol (natural spanish spice coloring)

salt to taste

white wine

fish broth

Cooking directions

Saute onions, green peppers and garlic in olive oil. Add pork,
ham, chicken and sausage and put aside. Steam the clams, mussels
and lobster and save the broth for cooking. In a large clay pot
or pan, saute shrimp and fish lightly. Add mixture of onion, pepper,
etc. Mix with tomatoes. Add 3 1/2 pounds rice (measure in cup and
use the same amount of rice as liquid, e.g., one cup of rice equals
one cup of liquid). Liquid should be a mixture of broth, white wine
and water in equal parts. Add spices. Let come to a boil on
high, add lobster and stone crabs. Cover tightly and turn to low
for 12 minutes. Open and add peas, chopped pimientos, clams and
mussels. Stir rice with ingredients. Adjust spices. Cover
tightly and let sit for 10 more minutes. Serve on platter. Garnish
with asparagus spears and pimientos.

Serving suggestion

Serve with a good dry white wine or sangria, a salad, and hard crusty
bread.

CHARLES CINNAMON
Director of Public Relations and Publicity

THE ZEV BUFMAN THEATRE PARTNERSHIP, LTD.

2980 McFARLANE ROAD, COCONUT GROVE, FLORIDA 33133 • 305-445-0575

ZEV BUFMAN'S SHRIMP

Leave shrimp unshelled, medium green color. Six pounds for six people. Sauce can be doubled or tripled.

Mix in sauce pan over low heat:

- 1/2 pound butter
- 3/4 cup of vegetable oil
- 12 oz bottle of chili sauce
- 3 tbs Worcestershire sauce
- 2 lemons, thin sliced
- ~~4 cloves of garlic, chopped~~
- 3 tbs of lemon juice
- 1 tbs of chopped parsley
- 2 tsp of paprika
- 2 tsp oregano
- 1 tsp cayenne pepper
- 1 tsp tabasco sauce
- 3 tbs of liquid smoke

Pour sauce over shrimp. Refrigerate for three hours or more; baste and turn every thirty minutes. Bake in 325° oven for thirty minutes; baste and turn every ten minutes. Serve in deep bowls for sauce with hot French bread; tear with fingers and dip into sauce. Serve with damp washcloths.

Exec. Offices:
2843 Pembroke Rd.
Hollywood, Fl. 33020

(305) 921-0881
1-800-327-9789

AMATEUR
GOLFERS' ASSOCIATION
AGA®

STUFFED SHELLS ALA AGA

2 LBS	RICOTTA CHEESE
8 OZ.	GRATED MOZZARELLA
2	EGGS (MED. LG)
2	TABLESPOONS PARSLEY, FRESH CHOPPED OR DEHYDRATED 1/4 TEASPOON
1/4	TEASPOON NUTMEG (TO TASTE OPTIONAL)
1 QT	PREPARED TOMATO SAUCE
3	TABLESPOONS ITALIAN CHEESE, GRATED
1 LB	LARGE SHELL MACARONI

MIX THE RICOTTA CHEESE, GRATED MOZZARELLA CHEESE, EGGS, PARSLEY, SALT AND NUTMEG (OPTIONAL), IN LARGE MIXING BOWL AND REFRIGERATE.

BOIL WATER IN A 2-3 GALLON POT ADDING 1/4 CUP OF OIL AND A HEAPING TABLESPOON OF SALT. WHEN WATER REACHES A BOIL, ADD THE SHELLS AND ALLOW THEM TO PARBOIL FOR 6-7 MINUTES UNTIL FIRM (ALDENTE)

STRAIN THE SHELLS INTO COLANDER AND RINSE THEM UNDER COLD WATER. AFTER SHELLS ARE RINSED, DRAIN THEM BY PLACING THEM UPSIDE DOWN INDIVIDUALLY ON PAPER TOWELS.

WHEN THE SHELLS HAVE THOROUGHLY DRAINED, WITH A TEASPOON, STUFF THE RICOTTA MIX INTO THE PRE-COOKED SHELLS. BE SURE NOT TO OVERSTUFF THE SHELLS.

NEXT, TAKE YOUR FAVORITE PREPARED TOMATO SAUCE AND COVER THE BOTTOM OF A LARGE BAKING PAN. PLACE THE SHELLS IN THE PAN WITH SPACE BETWEEN THEM AND COVER THEM WITH THE REMAINING TOMATO SAUCE AND SPRINKLE WITH GRATED CHEESE.

LAST BUT NOT LEAST, BE SURE TO COVER WITH ALUMINUM FOIL AND BAKE FOR 20-25 MINUTES AT 300 DEGREES. REMOVE PAN FROM OVEN AND LET SETTLE FOR 10 MINUTES AND SERVE.

SERVES 4-6 PEOPLE

AL CARROCCIA
PRESIDENT, AGA

REPERTORY COMPANY

CURRIED LAMB
(serves 6)

3 lbs lean Boneless Shoulder of Lamb trimmed of
   excess fat and cut into I 1/2 inch cubes
4 tbs Butter
2 tbs Vegetable Oil
3 cups Finely Chopped Onions
3 tbs Curry Powder
I tbs Finely Chopped Fresh Hot Chili Peppers
1/2 tsp Ground Allspice
2 tsp Salt
2 tsp Freshly Ground Black Pepper
I cup Coconut Milk fresh from the Coconut
I cup Coarsely Chopped Coconut
I cup Chicken Stock (fresh or canned)
I medium size Bay Leaf
2 tbs Strained Fresh Lime Juice

Pat the Lamb cubes completely dry with a paper towel. In a heavy
10-12" skillet, melt 2 tbs of the butter in the oil over moderate
heat. When the foam begins to subside, drop six or seven cubes of
lamb into the hot oil. Turn them with a spoon until the cubes are
brown on all sides. Make sure to regulate the heat so they color
richly and evenly without burning. As they color, transfer the
cubes onto a plate and brown the remaining Lamb similarly. Melt the
remaining 2 tbs of butter in the skillet. Add the onions. Stirring
frequently cook for about 5 minutes or until they are soft and
transparent, but not brown. Add the curry, chili peppers, allspice,
salt, and a few grindings of pepper. Stir constantly while
simmering for 2 to 3 minutes.

REPERTORY COMPANY

Return the Lamb and the juices that have accumulated around it to the skillet. Stir in the coconut, coconut milk, stock, and bay leaf, Bring to a boil over high heat. Reduce the heat to low and cover tightly. Simmer for I I/4 hours or until the lamb shows no resistance when pierced with the point of a sharp knife. Remove the bay leaf and stir in the lime juice. Season to taste.

To serve, mound the lamb in a deep heated platter or in a heated bowl. Pour the sauce over it. Curried lamb is traditionally accompanied by plain, boiled, or saffron rice and mango chutney.

Note: In Jamaica this curry is prepared with goat meat rather than lamb. You may substitute kid or goat if it is available.

Lago Mar Club

FORT LAUDERDALE, FLORIDA

PEANUT BUTTER PIE

INGREDIENTS:

    One (1) 9" pie shell
    Four (4) eggs
    1/8 teaspoon cream of tartar
    1/2 lb. of butter
    Two (2) cups powdered sugar
    2½ teaspoons vanilla
    One (1) 10 oz. jar peanut butter (Crunchy optional)

DIRECTIONS:

Bake pie shell according to package directions. Separate egg yolks/whites. In a cold stainless steel bowl or glass bowl (no plastic) whip egg whites with cream of tartar until they are peek. Set aside until later. In the same bowl or another bowl, whip (on medium speed) butter until creamy, adding sugar, vanilla and peanut butter.

When mixture is creamy, gradually add egg yolks until well blended. Take mixture and fold in egg whites. Fill pre-baked pie shell and chill. Chill for at least one (1) hour. Serve with your favorite topping.

KENNETH P. CARVER, C.E.C.

CALF SWEETBREADS WITH GRANNY SMITH APPLES,
CHESTNUTS AND FRESH TARRAGON

INGREDIENTS

2 Calf Sweetbreads
2 Apples
4 oz Chestnuts
1 cup Heavy Cream
1 Bunch Fresh Tarragon
(1/2 sprigs, 1/2 cleaned leaves)
4 oz clarified butter
1/4 cup white wine

2 oz White Vinegar
1 stalk celery-rough chop
1 med onion-rough chop
1 leek-cleaned, rough chop
flour seasoned with
salt and pepper
3 bay leaves

PROCEDURE

Soak sweetbreads in cold water with white vinegar for 30 minutes. Put the celery, onion, leek and bay leaves into a heavy saucepan filled with water and bring to a boil. Add the sweetbreads and slow simmer about 45 minutes, or until they're "sort of solid to the touch". Remove from water and cool. Slice sweetbreads into medallions. Lightly coat with seasoned flour. Peel, core and cut the apples into eigths.

Heat two saute pans with clarified butter. In one pan saute the apples, carefully browning them on each side. Set them aside. In the other pan, saute the sweetbreads, browning both sides. Deglaze the pan with white wine, then add the cream, the chestnuts and the tarragon leaves. Remove sweetbreads and arrange on a serving plate with apples. Reduce sauce until thick enough to coat "back of spoon". Nappe the sweetbreads with sauce. Garnish with tarragon sprigs and serve.

Chef Allen

19088 NE 29th Ave., North Miami Beach, Florida 33180

The Miami Herald

BROWARD COUNTY

1520 East Sunrise Boulevard
Fort Lauderdale, Florida 33304
(305) 527-8400

Fettuccine with Fresh Spinach and Tomatoes

1 pound fresh spinach, leaves only
1½ pounds fresh ripe tomatoes
1 small onion or one large shallot
1 tablespoon butter
1 clove garlic
2 or 3 fresh basil leaves (optional)
1½ cups heavy cream
Salt and pepper to taste
1 pound egg fettuccine
½ cup fresh-grated Parmesan or Fontina cheese

Rinse spinach in cold water until free of sand, dry completely with paper towels, then pile into mounds and cut across the leaves into ½-inch ribbons. Place tomatoes in boiling water for a minute, remove and peel. Cut in half horizontally and remove seeds. Cut into ½-inch cubes. Set aside spinach and tomatoes. Finely chop onion or shallot. Heat butter in a saucepan over medium heat. Add onion or shallot and sauté until limp. Add garlic and sauté 1 more minute: Add basil leaves and the heavy cream. Heat to just under a boil; reduce heat to barely simmering and let cream mixture reduce to 1 cup. Add salt and pepper to taste. Remove garlic and basil leaves if used.

Meanwhile, bring 4 to 6 quarts of water to boil in a large pot. Add 2 tablespoons salt. Add fettuccine and cook according to package directions. If you are using fresh pasta, it should cook in only a few minutes. Drain pasta; return to pot or place in a large bowl.

Add tomatoes to the cream and let steep for 1 minute. Pour mixture over the pasta. Add the spinach leaves and toss briefly. Add the grated cheese and toss again. Serve in soup plates with more cheese if desired.

Lucy Cooper
Miami Herald
Restaurant Critic
and Food Writer

Diplomat, Florida

LAMB FILLETS WITH PARSLEY AND MUSHROOMS

(To serve four people)

3/4 pounds parsley (about 3 large bunches)
  1 garlic clove
1/2 shallot
1/2 pounds wild mushrooms
  3 tablespoons of butter
1/2 cup of heavy cream
Salt and Pepper
  2 tablespoons of peanut oil
  4 six-ounce lamb fillets (cut from the saddle)

PREPARATIONS:

Cut or twist the stems of the parsley. Blanche the leaves in salted boiling water for six minutes, squeeze well and let dry on paper towels. Chop the garlic and the shallot. Clean the mushrooms and unless they are very small ones cut them into halves or quarters.

FINISHING:

Put 1½ tablespoons of butter into a frying pan with the chopped shallot. Cook over medium heat until the butter foams and then add parsley. Stir it with a fork to separate. Add the cream and bring to boil twice so that it thickens slightly and the parsley absorbs some of it. Season with salt and pepper, remove the pan from heat and set aside.

Heat 1 tablespoon of oil in a non-stick frying pan over high heat and add the mushrooms. When they have yielded their juices, add the remaining 1½ tablespoons of butter, the chopped garlic and salt and pepper. Mix well and let cook, stir over high heat, until the mushrooms are well browned. Remove from heat and set aside.

Heat the remaining 1 tablespoon of oil in a frying pan over medium heat. Salt and pepper the lamb fillets and saute for 4 minutes a side.

PRESENTATION:

Cut the fillets into thin slices. Arrange the slices of each fillet on an individual plate in the shape of a star. Put the parsley in the center and scatter the mushrooms over the meat.

Irving Cowan
Diplomat Resort and Country Clubs
Hollywood, Florida

RESORT AND COUNTRY CLUBS
3515 South Ocean Drive,
Hollywood, Florida 33019
Telephone: (305) 457-8111

CITY OF

FORT LAUDERDALE
FLORIDA

ROBERT O. COX
MAYOR

P. O. DRAWER 14250 · 33302

100 N. ANDREWS AVENUE
(305) 761-2245

June 23, 1987

<u>Mayorality Headache Stew</u>

Assemble following ingredients:

        Full portion (several hundred) irate
        homeowners
        1 Theatre developer
        1 Pinch of attorneys (escapees from
        Shakespearean solution)
        1 handful staff and department heads
        Small dose of stale zoning (preferably
        generations old)
        Bottle of rapacious sauce
        1 City Commission

Mix irate homeowners and attorneys in large room; add
attorneys and simmer 10-15 minutes.

Separately marinate developer in rapacious sauce for
several months, then add:

Puncture attorneys with large needle to let steam
escape.

Stir staff and stale zoning separately to bring out
uncertainty; squeeze City Commission to bring out
headache factor and combine all ingredients. Boil
for 1-1/2 hours.

Serves: Coral Ridge area

WARNING: Ingestion of large quantities may cause
         tremors. Be sure not to mix any of this
         recipe with "Four Laning Bayview Drive" stew.

AMERICAN EXPRESS TRAVEL RELATED SERVICES COMPANY, INC.
1876 N. UNIVERSITY DRIVE, SUITE 200, PLANTATION, FLORIDA 33322

ROBERT V. CREEKMORE
VICE PRESIDENT–S/E SALES & MARKETING
SOUTHERN REGION

For those of you who are health conscious, and fast paced introducing the superb:

SPINACH CASSEROLE

1   (10 oz.) package frozen, chopped spinach

1/2 cup tomato sauce

1   cup shredded cheddar cheese

1   cup sour cream

1   (4 oz.) can whole mushrooms, drained, salt to taste

1/4 teaspoon curry powder

Cook spinach according to package directions and drain very thoroughly. Add remaining ingredients. Place in 1 1/4 quart casserole. Bake at 350° for about 30 minutes, till heated through. Serves 4.

Enjoy -- and remember, its better to look good and feel good.

Bob Creekmore

POSH SQUASH

Having grown up in North Carolina, I can recall an abundance of fresh vegetables, many of which came from our own garden.

This recipe, which I proudly attribute to my Mom, is still one of my favorites. We hope you like it.

8-10 Medium to small yellow squash
2 large white onions
2 lemons
1/2 cup water (approximately)
1 1/2 cups grated cheddar cheese
1/2 clove of garlic
salt, pepper, Old Bay seasoning

Cut squash into 1/2 inch slices. Slice onions into thin rings. Place squash, onions, 1/2 cup water, juice from two lemons and sliced garlic along with a dash of 'Old Bay' into a large pot and cover. Simmer, stirring occasionally and add a little salt and pepper to taste. Drain off any excess water if necessary.

While the pot is still steaming hot, add the grated cheese slowly stirring all the while. Now place in a serving dish and sprinkle just a little 'Old Bay' on the top for color.

ENJOY!!

John Day

429 SEABREEZE BLVD. ● FORT LAUDERDALE, FLORIDA 33301 ● 305-467-6788

From the desk of
COUNTESS
HENRIETTA de HOERNLE

HERRING SALAD

1 Cup diced herring in wine filets
  Cup of beets
½ Cup boiled potatoes in jackets
¼ Cup of onion
¼ Cup chopped pickles
¼ Cup mayonnaise
1 Teaspoon mustard
  Seasoning

Mix well and let stand for two days in the refrigerator.

At Christmas and New Year's, you eat Herring Salad for good luck.

Countess Henrietta de Hoernle

DEN-CHOPS

6 Pork Chops
Butter (small amount)
1 Large Onion (chopped)
1 Tablespoon Flour

1 Cup Beef Bouillon (1 cube)
1 Rounded Tablespoon Regular Mustard
Salt & Pepper

Brown pork chops in a small amount of butter, remove them from the pan. Brown onion in the pan drippings until soft. Sprinkle flour over onions and stir. Stir in beef bouillon (made with one cube), mustard and salt and pepper to taste. Return the chops to the pan. Cover and simmer until tender (approx. an hour to an hour and one half). Add water if needed.

Christopher W. Denison

750 N.E. 7th Ave., P.O. Box 805, Dania, FL 33004 (305) 920-0622/920-4011

Telex: 316387 — DENSHIP / TeleFax: (305) 920-6553

Southern Wine and Spirits, Inc.

WHOLESALERS AND IMPORTERS OF FINE WINES AND LIQUORS
1600 N. W. 163rd STREET • MIAMI, FLORIDA 33169 • (305) 625-4171
BROWARD (305) 421-8060

MEL DICK
PRESIDENT
WINE DIVISION

Penne Con i Quattro Formoggi

4 oz. Fontina

4 oz. Parmesan

4 oz. Gorgonzola

4 oz. Bel Paese

1 cup bechamel, room temperature

½ teaspoon ground pepper.

Mix all ingredients in a saucepan and heat over very low temperature.

Cook pasta, after draining, mix pasta thoroughly with cheese sauce.

Thin sauce with cooking water, top with parmesan and ground pepper.

I was invited to the home of very dear friends, a Father and Son, who told me what they were planning on preparing for lunch. Once I saw the recipe, I asked if I could prepare the lunch. I have always found cooking to be a truly relaxing pass time. This has become one of my favorite Italian dishes .... Penne Con i Quattro Formoggi.

SUBSIDIARIES: COASTAL MERCHANDISING CO., DIVISION OF SOUTHERN WINE AND SPIRITS, INC. (MIAMI, FLA. 33169) • AMERICAN DISTRIBUTORS OF FLORIDA, INC. (JACKSONVILLE, FLA. 32203) • AMERICAN DISTRIBUTORS OF FLORIDA, INC. (ORLANDO, FLA. 32809) • CARBO, INCORPORATED (TAMPA, FLA. 33611) • WEST FLORIDA DISTRIBUTORS, INC. (PENSACOLA, FLA. 32501) • SOUTHERN WINE AND SPIRITS OF CALIFORNIA, INC. (HOLLYWOOD, CALIF. 91605) • SOUTHERN WINE AND SPIRITS OF NEVADA, INC. (LAS VEGAS, NEV. 89103) • SOUTHERN WINE AND SPIRITS OF NEVADA, INC. (RENO, NEV. 89431)

KATHARINE DICKENSON
TWELVE FORTY COCOANUT ROAD
BOCA RATON, FLORIDA 33432

Basil and Tomatoe Pasta

1 lb linguine
1 large handful fresh basil > chopped
5 large fresh red tomatoes > chopped
3/4 cup of virgin olive oil
1/4 cup of lemon juice
Sea Salt   Freshly ground pepper
Fresh garlic > at least four cloves minced
Chinese Hot and Spicy Oil - 1 teaspoon

Cook linguine al dente. Drain.
Toss remaining ingredients in a large
bowl & garnish with fresh basil leaves.
Serve at room temperature to
four persons. Great picnic food.

Katharine Dickenson

38

GULFSTREAM PARK RACING ASSOCIATION, INC.

DOUGLAS DONN
PRESIDENT

Harry M. Stevens Rice Pudding at Gulfstream Park

Douglas and Alice Donn

2 cups rice (Uncle Ben's converted)
4 cups water
1 whole cinnamon stick (broken in half)
peeling from one lemon
4 oz. butter
1 teaspoon salt
Simmer one-half hour

Add
1/2 gallon Half & Half
Simmer one hour stirring occasionally

Last two minutes
Add 1 1/2 cups sugar
1 1/2 teaspoons vanilla
1 1/2 cups raisins

Bring back to a boil
Add 4 eggs beaten (must be added slowly to avoid cooking)

George Dooley
President

P.O. Box 2
Miami, FL 33261-0002
Studios at
14901 N.E. Sesame Street
Miami, FL
(305) 949-8321

GENOISE (Pronounced Jhay-no-ahze)

Delicate sponge cake layers put together with the most delectable of cream fillings. One of the most famous and basic cakes of all Europe. When Catherine de Medicis came to France from Italy in 1533, she brought not only an appreciation of all the fine arts, but a retinue of chefs who introduced many fine Italian dishes, including Genoise, now called an "objet d'art of all Patisserie."

BAKE at 350° F. for 25 to 30 minutes. Makes two 8-inch round layers.
BEAT 1 cup eggs (about 5 medium) until light and fluffy.
ADD gradually 1 cup sugar, ½ teaspoon salt, 1 teaspoon vanilla,
BEAT until thick and lemon colored (about 10 min. at high speed)
FOLD IN, 1¼ cups sifted Pilsbury's Best Enriched Four, 2 tablespoons
      at a time, FOLD gently but thoroughly.
POUR into two 8-inch round layer pans, well greased and lined with
      waxed paper on the bottom.
BAKE in moderate over (350° F.) 25 to 30 minutes. Cool in pan on cake racks, Remove layers from pans and split to form four layers. Spread cool creme au beurre between layers and on sides of cake. Frost top with chocolate icing.

CREME AU BEURRE

Combine 3/4 cup sugar and 2 tablespoons cornstarch in saucepan. Mix well. Add 3 eggs (or 6 egg yolks). Beat until light and fluffy. (I beat this mixture at high speed for at least 5 to 10 minutes). Stir in 1½ cups milk; cook over medium heat until thick, stirring constantly. Remove from heat, add 1 teaspoon vanilla, cool. Blend in ½ cup soft creamed butter. (NOTE: I make a double recipe of the creme au beurre to cover and fill the cake more generously).

. . . . Continued

George Dooley
President

P.O. Box 2
Miami, FL 33261-0002
Studios at
14901 N.E. Sesame Street
Miami, FL
(305) 949-8321

GENOISE   (Continued)

CHOCOLATE ICING

Cream 2 tablespoons butter or margarine. Blend in 1 cup sifted confectioner's sugar. Add 1 or ½ small egg; beat well. Blend in 1 square (1 oz) melted chocolate and ½ teaspoon vanilla. Beat until smooth.

Frost and fill the cake with the Creme au Beurre leaving the top of the cake bare for the Chocolate Icing. Spread chocolate icing on top. Be sure that the cake, the creme au beurre and chocolate icing are cool. Store cake in refrigerator.

Submitted by,

George W. Dooley

ZUCCHINI ALLA PARMIGIANA

1 pound tomatoes
1/2 small onion, thinly sliced
1 tablespoon butter or margarine
6 tablespoons olive or salad oil
Pinch of basil
2 cloves minced garlic

Salt and pepper to taste
8 small zucchini
1/4 cup flour
2 tablespoons grated Parmesan cheese
1/2 pound Mozzarella cheese, thinly sliced

Peel tomatoes. Cut into pieces; remove seeds. Sauté onion in combined butter and 1 tablespoon of the olive oil until soft but not brown. Add tomatoes, basil, salt, pepper, and chopped garlic. Simmer uncovered, stirring occasionally, for 30 minutes. Meanwhile, cut off ends of zucchini. Cut in half lengthwise. Coat lightly with flour. Saute in 4 tablespoons of the olive oil until golden brown; drain on absorbent paper. With remaining tablespoon of oil, coat the bottom of a 1 1/2-quart casserole. Place alternate layers of zucchini, prepared tomato sauce, Parmesan cheese, and Mozzarella cheese, ending with Mozzarella cheese topped with sauce in casserole. Bake uncovered at 350° for 30 minutes or until zucchini is tender.
Serves 4 to 6.

Judy Drucker

Judy Drucker

BAKED PORK CHOPS

(Serves 8)

Sprinkle pan with 1½ packages of Herb Rice. Place 8
<u>dryed</u> Butterfly Boneless Pork Chops on top. Cover each
chop with a dab of catsup and a slice of onion. Add
2 cans of Beef Consumme'. Seal tightly with foil and
bake at 350° for 1½ hours.

Very Easy and Very Good.

For those of you who work and have a one year old son,
this is a great recipe to have for company!!

Jeanne Evert Dubin

Jeanne Evert Dubin

ALAMO RENT A CAR, INC.

POST OFFICE BOX 22776

1401 SOUTH FEDERAL HIGHWAY

FORT LAUDERDALE, FLORIDA 33335

TELEPHONE (305) 527-6550

TELEX 803 926

MICHAEL S. EGAN
PRESIDENT
CHIEF EXECUTIVE OFFICER

HEADING FOR GOURMET SENILITY AT 47

I once, in the fast receding days of youth, taught a course in classical cuisine and fine wine and was an ardent practitioner of the culinary arts. But the truth is, I started in hamburgers as a grillman in my teens and hamburgers are today my lot - or perhaps my soul's secret choice. Lunches are most times a hamburger, fast if needed, and reliable, like an old friend. Worse, if I have the choice, I find myself ordering a hamburger in great restaurants (and choosing to go there because I can). I just get so sick of sauces and artfully arranged carrots.

~~There are essentially two kinds of hamburgers. Those eaten with a~~ bun and those eaten without. In the latter category the world's best are to be found at "Billy's" on about 51st Street and 1st Avenue in New York City. As for hamburgers eaten on a bun...

HAMBURGERS
A LONG-WINDED RECIPE

Hamburger meat - fresh ground beef with 28% - 30% fat content. Don't buy lean ground round, it tastes like shoe leather. Use fresh (not frozen) meat.

Hamburgers are simply much better when griddled (frying pan) than when broiled or barbecued. The meat stays moist and the interaction of the fat cooking and the lean meat cooking establishes the elementary flavor.

Hamburger patties must be approximately round; square and oblong don't griddle evenly. Don't make them in a press; they're better by hand with uneven edges. The size of the patty is critical. The initial raw size when formed should be the diameter of the bun or roll on which they're served and no more than 3/8" thick. (Most people make hamburgers way too thick and way too big). A great hamburger weighs about 3 - 4 ounces; 4 to 5 to a pound.

Hamburgers should be griddled on a medium hot frying surface, covered with a moderate lubricating layer of grease. Butter, Fleishman's Margarine, and Crisco oil all work. Don't use burned margarine or butter or corn oil. Most hamburgers take about 4 to 5 minutes to cook. Don't dry them out. The best flavor, however, is not medium rare, which hasn't integrated the fat and the lean sufficiently. The best doneness is a step above medium rare with a dash of pink left in the meat. Hamburger seasoning is salt and pepper after the surface has been cooked. Add nothing to the raw meat.

Hamburgers, thus cooked, must be served on very fresh hamburger buns or rolls, approximately the diameter of a bun or perhaps a little smaller. Anything larger than a regular bun is too large. It eats sloppy and the hamburger is too large to cook well.

Hamburgers are the natural platform for one kind of food - onions. Griddled onions, though not always wanted, are the single largest olfactory plus that can be given a cooked sandwich. (Including hot dogs from our own Hot Dog Heaven - a 10 on anybody's list - and steak hoagies (haven't had one since my days at Fort Leonard Wood, Mo., where I learned the lesson I just taught you about fried onions from the guy who walked through our basic training barracks selling "real food" from town). If raw onions are used, a 1/4" slice from the middle of a sweet onion is the only choice. The onions of choice are: 1st - Vadalia, 2nd - Maui, and 3rd -Bermuda.

Hamburgers are ultimately the natural partner for Heinz Ketchup - don't bother with any other brand. And, if mustard is your druthers, Dijon by Grey Poupon is best. And now...

THE BEST HAMBURGER

Hamburger   4 sliced dill pickle chips
Slice of raw onion   More salt and a little ketchup
A fresh roll of some distinction, buns are a little mundane.

THE SECOND BEST HAMBURGER

Chop a handful of onion and griddle in oil with the hamburger on top of the onion (this takes a little longer). Turn the hamburger so the onions are on top and add a slice of Kraft Olde English cheese over the top of the onions. Fry an egg with the yolk broken (soft but not runny) and put on the hamburger over the cheese. Serve on a fresh hamburger bun with a little ketchup.

A HAMBURGER RARELY SEEN

Hamburger
Mixture of cream cheese & chopped green olive stuffed w/pimiento
Toasted bun

SOMETHING CLOSE TO A HAMBURGER TO DIE FOR

A raw slice of filet mignon cut 3/8" thick in the shape of a hamburger and cooked exactly like a hamburger, medium rare. Top with a teaspoon heaping full of light grey caviar, either Beluga or Mallasol. Serve on a warm roll, slightly less large than a hamburger bun.

For dinner parties, this dish is almost as good when a filet is roasted, medium rare, and sliced to about 1/4" thick, then topped with caviar and served on a white dinner roll (2" roll).

Michael S. Egan, President
Museum of Art, Fort Lauderdale

Hans Eichmann

COQUILLES ST. JACQUES
AUX POIREAUX ET TRUFFES

12	Fresh Scallops
½ C.	Fish Stock
1 C.	Heavy Cream
1 Oz.	Truffles, julienned
1	Leek, julienned
1	Shallot, finely chopped
	Salt and White Pepper, to taste

Place fish stock and shallots in pan. Reduce
until consistency of syrup. Add heavy cream
and scallops. Cook lightly. Remove scallops.
Reduce cream mixture. Add salt and pepper,
truffles, and leek. Cook for one minute.

Place scallops on plate and cover with sauce.

Good Luck

Props.

Chris Evert

500 Northeast 25th Street
Wilton Manors, Florida 33305-1135

"Inside-Out" Chocolate Bundt Cake

First of all......choose a cold, rainy day. Preheat your
oven to 350°. Grease Bundt pan completely with shortening.

    1 pkg. (4 ounce) Chocolate Jello Instant
        Pudding and Pie Filling
    1 pkg. (18.25 ounce) Duncan Hines Deluxe
        Devil's Food or Chocolate Cake Mix
    1 pkg. (12 ounce) Baker's Semi-Sweet Chocolate
        flavored chips
    1 3/4 cups homogenized milk
    2 eggs
    1 cup chopped pecans

Combine pudding mix, cake mix, chocolate chips, milk and eggs
in a very large bowl. Mix by hand until well blended - about
two minutes. Fold in chopped pecans.

Bake in greased Bundt pan in pre-heated 350° oven for 50-55
minutes, or until cake springs back when lightly pressed
with finger. Cool for thirty minutes in the pan. Remove
from pan.

        The cake is so rich, you really don't
        need frosting. You may serve with
        vanilla ice cream or LeCreme whipped
        cream, if desired.

The cake can be cut in quarters and frozen so small portions
may be used at a time.

The delicious aroma wafting from your oven will weaken the
willpower of the strictest dieter.

After the feast, you must pay the penalty.....maybe three
sets of singles on a hot, sunny court.

Enjoy
Chris Evert

Leonard L. Farber

RED CABBAGE

This Red Cabbage is best served with "Sauerbraten" (spiced marinated beef) and "Knodel" (light weight dumplings).

INGREDIENTS:

3 - 4 lbs. of fresh red cabbage
1 onion
1 lb. of sour apples
1 - 2 tbsp. of goose fat
1 - 3 tbsp. of jelly (apple, strawberry, etc.)
1 - 2 tbsp. of vinegar (to taste)
5 cloves
3 - 5 Wacholderbeinen - Currant berries
1 bay laurel leaf
1 glass of red wine
Caraway seeds, salt, paprika & pepper to taste

PREPARATION:

1. Wash and shred the red cabbage, pin the onion with the cloves, dice the apples finely.

2. Combine the ingredients except the apples and fill up with water half of the cabbage. Cook until tender (about 300°) for one hour.

3. Add the apples and let them cook with the cabbage another half hour.

4. Take out the onion with the cloves and the bay laurel leaf, pour out the water.

5. Ready to serve.

MARINATED SEA SCALLOPS WITH SMOKED SALMON

(Serves 4)

16 jumbo sea scallops
1/4 cup olive oil
1 tablespoon white vinegar
2 tablespoons chopped fresh dill
Salt and pepper to taste
12 ounces thinly sliced smoked Norwegian Salmon
Lemon slices and sprigs of fresh dill, for garnish

In a medium saucepan, bring 1 quart water to boiling. Add scallops and cook until opaque, about 2 minutes. Drain well. Place scallops in a small bowl with olive oil, lemon juice, vinegar, dill and salt and pepper to taste. Cover and refrigerate several hours or overnight.

Arrange salmon slices slightly overlapping on four plates. Top with marinated scallops. Garnish with lemon slices and sprigs of fresh dill.

Buenaventura Fernandez
Buenaventura Fernandez
Executive Chef

Pier66

Hotel and Marina / 2301 S.E. 17th Street / Fort Lauderdale, FL 33316
Telephone 305 525-6666

BAKED STUFFED CLAMS

2 1/2 lbs	Chopped Clams (including Juice)
1/2 cup	Vegetable Oil
1/4 oz	Ground Oregano Leaves
1/2 cup	Grated Parmesan Cheese
6 oz	Italian Bread Crumbs

Mix first four Ingredients, then add Bread Crumbs; Mix Well. Stuff in Clam Shell; Broil 7-10 minutes or until golden brown. Makes approximately 40 Clams.

By Carmine Ferrante

Carmine Ferrante

1536 Cordova Road (Off 17th Street Causeway) □ Fort Lauderdale, Florida 33316 □ 525-CLAM

CARRIBEAN SALMON

1 large can of salmon
1 large green pepper and 1 small red pepper (if in season)
1 large onion (chop fine)
2 or 3 stalks of celery (chop medium)
½ garlic clove (chop fine)
3½ tablespoons of olive oil
1 24oz can of tomato sauce
1 small can of tomato paste
1 teaspoon of oregano
1 teaspoon of thyme
½ teaspoon of salt
½ tablespoon peppercorn (ground)

2 cups of rice

Cook rice separately

Onions, green and red peppers and celery saute in olive oil
for 2 minutes
add garlic clove (stir for 2 minutes)
add seasonings
Stir in salmon chunks over medium heat for 10 minutes
add tomato sauce and paste (simmer for 6 minutes)
Cover and remove from heat for 5 minutes.
Serve over rice.   Serves 4

Geoff Fisher
(Jazz Director)

SONNY'S MIDNIGHT DELIGHT......AKA....DOGS AND SHROOMS

TAKE TWO HOT DOGS AND SLICE THEM INTO ONE HALF INCH SEGMENTS.

PLACE IN POT WITH ONE CAN OF CAMPBELLS CHUNKY MUSHROOM SOUP.

ADD ONE SMALL CAN OF MUSHROOM CAPS OR FRESH MUSHROOMS IF DESIRED.

ADD ONE PINCH OF POWDERED GARLIC AND PARSLEY, AND ONE EIGTH OF A
STICK OF BUTTER.
STIR WITH A WHISK WHILE HEATING OVER A LOW FLAME. SERVE HOT WITH
STONE WHEAT CRACKERS.

SONNY FOX

2741 N. 29th Avenue • Suite 300 • Hollywood, Florida 33020 • Dade (305) 944-1956 • Broward (305) 925-7117 • Palm Beach (305) 655-0994

MR. AND MRS. R. M. GARDNER
2412 NORTH EAST 14TH STREET
FORT LAUDERDALE, FLORIDA 33304

Lemon Meringue Pie (Joyce's Mother's)

6 eggs---separate yolks and whites of five; into the
yolks add the whole 6th egg. Beat yolks, add one cup of
sugar and 3 level tablsp. of flour, 1/2 tsp salt.

Put juice of 2 lemons into a cup;fill to the brim with
water; add this to mixture; put in double boiler

Cook, stirring frequently till it thickens, then add 1/4
stick butter.

Beat 5 whites till stiff; add 4 level tblsp. powdered sugar;
put in dabs on top; brown in very hot oven 1-3- minutes.

Use your favorite pie crust.

Joyce T. Gardner

Schizophrenic Tuna

RIP OPEN

Take one can of Bumble-bee Chunk Light tuna in spring water — it would help to know if the tuna was neurotic (the meat is firmer) (Accept NO SUBSTITUTE)

Take 2 eggs, boil them violently and slash them into smaller bits.

GRAB With a very sharp knife — cut 2 slices of Vidalia onions and chop them finely.

Repeat with a medium size green pepper.

add to Taste: dill weed and medium ground black pepper PLUS

Add 2¾ dollops of Hellman's mayonnaise.

throw them together and stir. this

Serve on Cuban crackers and with Monterey wine, or Seagrams wine cooler, OUTFIT: Outfit: it depends on who is coming for dinner. Use your own judgment, but think TUNA.

"OR"

~~NORMAL~~

~~Schizophrenia~~

~~Other~~: a very elegant contemporary space, dim lights, and a one foot taper candle. Play a tape by Rocio Jurado or Esther Satterfield or your choice

Wear your most provocative outfit (but think TUNA.) Low lights - guaranteed to ~~produce~~ induce memorable dreams.

Fernando Garcia
Miami, Fl.

800 Brickell Avenue
Miami, Florida 33131
305/350-1825

Hugh E. Gentry
Chairman and
Chief Executive Officer

CORN BREAD

1 package cornbread mix
1 small onion
½ green pepper
1 can corn niblets
Tabasco

Prepare cornbread mix according to package instructions, with egg and milk. Add to batter: 3 dashes of tabasco sauce, 1 small diced onion, ½ minced green pepper and one can of corn niblets. Add flour as necessary to thicken mixture, and bake in a 350° oven for 25 minutes.

Hugh Gentry

Trivest, Inc.

2665 South Bayshore Drive
Suite 801
Miami, Florida 33133
Tel (305) 858-2200

CREECH ORCHARD WALNUT CARROT CAKE

2	cup	flour	2	cups grated carrots	
1	tsp	baking soda	1	cup raisins	
1	tsp.	baking powder	1	cup chopped Creech	

2   cup   flour
1   tsp   baking soda
1   tsp. baking powder
1/2   tsp. salt
4   tsp. cinnamon
1-1/2 cup sugar
1   cup melted margarine, salad
         oil or butter
1   tsp. vanilla
3   eggs

2   cups grated carrots
1   cup raisins
1   cup chopped Creech
      Orchard Hartley
      English Walnuts (or
      other fine quality
      walnuts)
1/2 tsp. cloves
1/2 tsp. nutmeg
1/2 tsp. allspice

Mix all ingredients (do not overmix) and pour into greased
Bundt pan. Bake 1-1-1/4 hours in 350 degree oven.

Let cool and use your favorite powdered sugar or cream cheese
icing.

To decorate, fill a votive candle holder with flowers.
Surround cake platter with additional flowers and greenery.

NOTE: In order to authentically prepare this cake, one must
become friends with Brev and Sara Jane Creech who live in
Chico, California!

Phillip & Judy George
Miami, Florida

APPLE PANCAKE

2   RED DELICIOUS APPLES, PEELED, CORED AND
     SLICED

1/2 POUND BUTTER,

BATTER:

2   CUP FLOUR, 1 CUP MILK, 6 EGGS

1/2 TEASPOON SALT

DASH VANILLA

1/2 TABLESPOON CINNAMON AND 1 1/2 TABLESPOON
     SUGAR MIXED TOGETHER

PLACE FLOUR AND SALT IN THE BOWL OF AN ELECTRIC MIXER. ADD MILK
UNTIL IT FORMS A PASTE. THEN ADD (2) EGGS AND MIX UNTIL SMOOTH.
TURN OFF MIXER AND ADD REMAINING EGGS AND VANILLA. LET SIT FOR
(20) MINUTES.

PREHEAT OVEN TO 425 DEGREES. CLARIFY 1/2 POUND OF BUTTER BY
MELTING IN A SAUCE PAN. TURN OFF THE HEAT AND LET IT SIT FOR A
FEW MINUTES. SKIM OFF FOAM FROM THE TOP AND DISCARD. THEN SKIM
THE LAYER OF OIL AND SET ASIDE TO USE LATER.

MIX TOGETHER CINNAMON AND SUGAR. YOU WILL NEED (2) 10-INCH
SAUCE PANS, OR MAKE (1) PANCAKE AT A TIME, USING 1/2 THE BATTER
AND 1/2 THE APPLES.

FOR EACH PANCAKE PLACE (2) OUNCES CLARIFIED BUTTER IN YOUR PAN
AND SAUTE THE SLICED APPLES FOR (1) MINUTE. TURN ON THE MIXER
AND BLEND THE BATTER FOR (10) SECONDS---JUST ENOUGH TO MIX. ADD
(6) OUNCES OF BATTER PER PANCAKE, INTO PAN. TILT THE PAN AND
USING A RUBBER SPATULA, SMOOTH EXCESS BATTER AROUND SIDES OF THE
PAN.

FLIP THE PANCAKE AFTER IT IS BROWN ON THE BOTTOM. SPRINKLE (1)
TABLESPOON OF THE CINNAMON SUGAR ON THE PANCAKE AND PUT IN
PREHEATED OVEN TO BAKE FOR (10) MINUTES OR UNTIL PUFFED AND GOLDEN
BROWN. SERVE IMMEDIATELY WITH LINGONBERRIES OR OTHER PRESERVES.

MAKES TWO PANCAKES.

NORBERT M. GOLDNER

JOSE A. GONZALEZ, JR.
JUDGE

BLACK BEAN SOUP
"FRIJOLES NEGROS"

```
1    pound dry black beans
1/4  pound ham hocks
1    cup olive oil
1/2  cup vinegar
2    large onions, chopped
3    green peppers, chopped
3    large cloves garlic, finely chopped
3    bay leaves
1    tablespoonful salt
3    quarts water
```

1. Wash the dry beans thoroughly and pour all the water off.

2. Soak the beans and ham hocks overnight in 3 quarts of water. The water will turn black, but you will use this water to cook the beans.

3. In a frying pan saute' lightly the onions, green peppers, and garlic in the olive oil. When onions are limp but not brown add the onions, peppers, garlic to the black beans and ham hocks.

4. Add salt and bay leaves.

5. Bring to a boil, reduce heat and cook slowly over low heat until the beans are very tender and the liquid has thickened.

6. Add the 1/2 cup vinegar to the beans a few minutes before serving.

7. Serve over cooked white rice and top with chopped onions. Serves six.

* * * * * * * * * * * * * * * * *

This is my mother's receipe slightly modified to my taste.

If the beans are allowed to stand overnight after cooking they will thicken and their flavor will improve.

59

Florida House of Representatives

Elaine Gordon
Representative, 102nd District

Reply to:
☐ 12100 NE 16th Avenue
   North Miami, FL 33161
   (305) 895-1066
☐ 220 The Capitol
   Tallahassee, FL 32399-1300
   (904) 488-7088

Committees

Appropriations
   HRS/Criminal Justice Subcommittee,
   Chairperson
Regulatory Reform
   Business Regulation Subcommittee,
   Chairperson
Regulated Industries & Licensing
Criminal Justice
Health Care
Rules & Calendar

Low Calorie "Bananas Foster"

	calories
1 Banana	100
3 TBS Carey's imitation maple syrup	15
2 TBS Sugar Twin brown sugar	10
2 TBS Orange Liqueur	10
1 dollop cool whip	20
Butter flavored Pam	
Teflon frying pan	
Total Calories	155

Cut banana lenthwise and in half
Spray pan with Pam
Brown banana on both sides and remove from Pan
Combine syrup, sugar and liqueur in pan and cook until
   bubbly and all ingredients are blended (2 or 3 minutes).
Return bananas to pan and coat them well with the
   mixture.
Arrange bananas on plate in a star pattern, pour syrup
   over them, and put dollop of cool whip in center.
Serve immediately so that cool whip won't melt.

CARY GOTT
Executive Vice President
Winemaster

MAYONNAISE KISSES

When I was a child, my parents had me pass these delicious
hors d'oeuvres to guests at cocktail parties they frequently
hosted for Modesto "Society". I usually passed them until one
or two were remaining on the tray. Then I would return to the
kitchen for more (and, of course, eat what was left on the tray).

A few years ago, I gave them the name 'Mayonnaise Kisses', and
in honor of them, I obtained a personalized license plate for my
Porsche that reads "MANAZE".

I love to eat them--they are outstanding!

Best Foods or Hellman's Mayonnaise (do not substitute)
White boiling onions - 1" diameter
Paprika
Regular white bread

Use a 2" round cookie cutter to cut out 4 rounds per slice of bread
with no crusts.

Peel and thinly slice (1/8"-1/4") the onions, and put one onion
round on top of each round of the white bread.

Put a dollop of Mayonnaise on top of the onion, and sprinkle lightly
with paprika.

Preheat broiler.

Broil on cookie sheet 6"-8" from heat (about 1-2 minutes).

Serve warm.

Cary Gott

United States Senate
WASHINGTON, DC 20510

ORANGE DESSERT SQUARES

CAKE:

2/3 c. sugar
1/2 c. butter or margarine
2 eggs separated
2 c. self rising flour
3/4 c. milk
4 tsp. grated orange rind

Cream butter and sugar, add egg yolks and beat until fluffy. Add flour alternatively with milk at low speed, beginning and ending with flour.

Beat egg whites until stiff but not dry. Fold egg whites and orange rind into batter. Pour batter into a greased 13 x 9 inch baking pan. Bake at 375 for 20 to 25 minutes until golden brown.

ORANGE SAUCE:

2/3 c. sugar
1 tbs. cornstarch
1 c. boiling water
1/4 tsp. salt
1 tsp. butter or margarine
4 tsp. grated orange rind
1/2 c. orange juice

In a small saucepan mix together sugar, cornstarch and salt; pour boiling water over mixture, stirring constantly. Cook over moderate heat until mixture boils and thickens. Add butter, orange rind and juice.

Serve squares with orange sauce. Makes 15 to 18 servings.

United States Senator

Mable's Chocolate Cake

    1/2 cup crisco
    2 cups sugar
    1/2 teaspoon salt
    1/2 cup cocoa
    2 eggs
    2 cups flour
    1-1/2 teaspoons vanilla
    1/2 teaspoon baking powder
    1-1/2 teaspoons soda
    3/4 cup buttermilk
    1 cup boiling water

Cream crisco and sugar, add cocoa and eggs. Add soda and baking powder to buttermilk and beat until well blended. Alternate flour and buttermilk mixture with crisco and sugar...at very last, add one cup boiling water. (May add one cup nuts.) Bake at 350° for 25 minutes.

Frosting

    1 stick butter
    1 small can pet milk
    2 cups sugar
    1 6 oz. pack chocolate chips

Mix all ingredients together in pan...bring to full boil for about two minutes...beat well...let cool before icing cake.

Submitted by: _John Hambrick_____
             John Hambrick, Anchor/Reporter

PEPPER CURED SALMON

LIME AND HORSERADISH SORBET

SERVES 10 PEOPLE

Lime and Horseradish Sorbet

Lime Juice	3 oz.
Simple Syrup	3 cups
Grated Horseradish	1½ oz
Egg Whites	1 ea.
Lime Zest	of 1 lime

Combine the lime juice, simple syrup, horseradish and lime zest. (26 brick).
Whip the egg whites to a light froth and add. Pour into a ice cream machine
and freeze. Store at -10°f and shape.

Pepper Cured Salmon

Salmon filet	2# 4 oz.
Salmon Cure:	
Refined Sugar	5 oz.
Brown Sugar	5 oz.
Salt	7 oz.
Allspice	1 oz.
Nutmeg	½ oz.
Ginger	¼ oz.
Mace	¼ oz.
Pickling Spice	1 oz.
Mustard Seed	1 oz.
Dill Seed	2 oz.
Dry Mustard	1 oz.
Ground Black Pepper	4 oz.

Combine all dry ingredients and pack around boneless,skinless salmon filet
for 3 days. After curing time of three days wash filet towel dry and dredge
with ground black pepper, rest for 4 hours and brush off excess pepper,
slice thinly - 3 slices per portion.

SITE OF THE 1987 PGA CHAMPIONSHIP
400 AVENUE OF THE CHAMPIONS, PALM BEACH GARDENS, FLORIDA 33418-3698 — 305/627-2000

Pepper Cured Salmon Continued

Base:

Belgium Endive	20 leaves
Julienne Red Pepper	1 ea.
Julienne Cucumber	1 ea.
Julienne Diacon	1 ea.
Julienne Carrott	1 ea.

Julienne Marinade

Rice Vinegar	3 oz.
Sugar Refined	3 oz.
Salt	To taste
White Pepper	To taste
Worcester	Dash
Tobasco	Dash

Whip all ingredients together, toss julienne ingredients and remove from excess marinade.

For presentation center dinner plate with a nest of marinated julienne vegetables. At the upper left hand portion of the plate flair two leaves of Belgium endive with a quenelle of sorbet in each. On the right side of the nest place 3 slices, folded, of pepper cured salmon. Garnish the presentation with lime segments, fresh crown dill and chive buds.

Raymond S Hammer

ROAST LAMB WITH PEPPERCORN CRUST

3 tablespoons crushed dried peppercorns, an equal mix of white,
    black, and green
1 tablespoon fresh rosemary leaves, or 1½ teaspoons dried
½ cup fresh mint leaves
5 garlic cloves, crushed
⅓ cup raspberry vinegar *
¼ cup Oriental soy sauce
½ cup dry red wine
1 boned but untied leg of lamb, about 5 pounds (weighed after boning)
2 tablespoons prepared Dijon-style mustard

1. Combine 1 tablespoon of the crushed peppercorns, the
rosemary, mint, garlic, vinegar, soy sauce and red wine in a
shallow bowl. Marinate the lamb in a mixture for eight hours,
turning occasionally.
2. Remove roast from marinade and drain; reserve marinade.
Roll the roast,. tying it with kitchen twine.
3. Preheat oven to 350 F.
4. Spread mustard over meat and pat 2 tablespoons of crushed
peppercorns into the mustard. Set the roast in a shallow roasting
pan just large enough to hold it comfortably and pour reserved
marinade carefully around but not over roast.
5. Bake for 1½ hours, or 18 minutes per pound, basting
occasionally. Roast will be medium rare. Bake for another 10 to
15 minutes for well-done meat. Let roast stand for 20 minutes
before carving. Serve pan juices in gravy boat along with lamb.
    6 to 8 portions

*available in specialty food stores, like Macy's

Guten Appetit !
Duane Hanson
this is how we celebrat Arbor Day.

EGGPLANT ITALIAN

Ingredients

One Eggplant
8oz Cooked Broad Noodles
2 cups Cut-Up Tomatoes
1 cup Thinly-Sliced Green Peppers
½ cup Bouillon
1 cup Grated Sharp Cheddar Cheese
¼ cup butter
Flour
Soda Cracker Crumbs
Salt & Pepper To Taste

Preparation

Slice Eggplant into ½" strips and parboil 10 minutes. In a 2 quart greased casserole dish layer the Noodles, Tomatoes and Green Peppers. Sprinkle Flour to cover the layer, adding a dash of Salt & Pepper to taste. Place the Eggplant Slices over the top of the layered ingredients, and pour ½ cup Bouillon over the top. Sprinkle the Grated Sharp Cheddar Cheese over the Bouillon, adding Flour, Salt & Pepper to cover. Dot with Butter. Sprinkle the Soda Cracker Crumbs over the entire top. Bake for one hour in a 350 degree oven. Serves six.

From,

MARY HART

CAPS PLACE, INC. d/b/a
CAPS PLACE ISLAND RESTAURANT
SEAFOOD SPECIALTIES SINCE THE 1920'S
Dock Located - 2765 N.E. 28th Court
Lighthouse Point, Florida 33064
Mailing Add. - Suite 110, 4081 N. Federal Hwy.
Pompano Beach, Florida 33064
Office (305) 941-2348   Restaurant (305) 941-0418

RECIPE FOR OBTAINING THE HEART FROM A SABAL PALM

If you have ever eaten fresh hearts of palm salad you may
have considered harvesting your own. This is no small task.
Hopefully the steps below will guide you. Since this is the
state tree of Florida you know doubt have a picture of this
tree proudly displayed in your home or office. If for some
reason you don't please get one as there are several types
of palms, and we do not want you axing the wrong tree.

INGREDIENTS:

One swamp
All terrain vehicles
Pair of heavy rubber boots
Machete or weapon of your choice
Heavy Ax
Men with strong backs
Two sabal palm trees

METHOD:

The first step in this recipe is using the proper equipment
hence the need for a all terrain vehicle capable of
maneuvering in high water (no your BMW isn't that well
made). You may wish to consider an additional vehicle in the
likely event that you will get bogged down in the swamp. Be
sure to be wearing those heavy rubber boots (1/4 inch thick
at least) since swamping areas are generally infested with
rattlesnakes (this is where your machete or weapon of your
choice will come in handy). The vital ingredient to this
recipe is several strong backs since the trunk of a mature
palm is quite thick and heavy. If you do in fact succeed in
cutting down the tree, (and I have my doubts) the heart is
located at the top. Better still bring the whole tree to the
restaurant and we will extract the heart for you, after all
if you have gone to this much trouble it's the least we can
do. Remember the final ingredient and the golden rule to
cutting down any tree ALWAYS PLANT TWO IN IT'S PLACE.

RON HERSEY'S MESQUITE GRILLED SWORDFISH

ONE <u>FRESH</u> SWORDFISH FILLET
ONE BOTTLE OF ITALIAN SALAD DRESSING
ONE ALUMINUM FOIL CAKE PAN
TWO MESQUITE CHIPS

SOAK THE MESQUITE CHIPS IN WATER OVERNIGHT. (YOU WANT SMOKE, NOT A FLAME!). PRE-HEAT YOUR BAR-B-QUE GRILL ON "MEDIUM" SETTING. EMPTY ENTIRE BOTTLE OF ITALIAN SALAD DRESSING INTO ALUMINUM CAKE PAN AND ON TOP OF SWORDFISH STEAKS. (ONE STEAK PER PERSON). COVER AND GRILL UNTIL FISH IS LIGHT AND FLAKY, TURNING ONLY ONCE.

BE CAREFULL NOT TO OVERCOOK, AS FISH TENDS TO BECOME RUBBERY.

THIS METHOD ALSO WORKS WELL WITH FRESH DOLPHIN, SHARK OR YOUR FAVORITE TYPE OF FISH. FRESH SHRIMP OR SCALLOPS ALSO TASTE GREAT WHEN PREPARED THIS WAY.

RON HERSEY
NEWS DIRECTOR
MAN OF A THOUSAND VOICES

2741 N. 29th Avenue • Suite 300 • Hollywood, Florida 33020 • Dade (305) 944-1956 • Broward (305) 925-7117 • Palm Beach (305) 655-0994

69

Chocolate Mousse Heatter

6 PORTIONS

It has been said that chocolate is the sexiest of all flavors. If so, this is the sexiest of all desserts.

8 ounces semisweet, bittersweet, or
    extra-bittersweet chocolate
1 tablespoon dry instant coffee
⅓ cup boiling water
5 eggs (graded large or extra-large), separated
Pinch of salt

Coarsely chop or break up the chocolate and place it in a small, heavy saucepan. Dissolve the coffee in the boiling water and pour it over the chocolate. Place over low heat and stir occasionally with a small wire whisk until smooth. Remove from the heat and set aside to cool for about 5 minutes.

Meanwhile, in the small bowl of an electric mixer, beat the egg yolks at high speed for 3 to 4 minutes until they are pale lemon-colored. Reduce the speed to low, gradually add the slightly warm chocolate, and beat, scraping the bowl with a rubber spatula. Beat only until smooth. Remove from the mixer.

Add the salt to the egg whites and beat with clean beaters only until they hold a definite shape but not until they are stiff or dry

Without being too thorough, gently fold about one-quarter of the beaten whites into the chocolate mixture, then fold in a second quarter, and finally fold the chocolate into the remaining whites, folding only until no whites show.

Gently transfer the mousse to a wide pitcher and pour it into six large wine glasses, each with about a 9-ounce capacity. Do not fill the glasses too full; leave generous headroom on each. (I always prepared this mousse in individual glasses and thought it had to be best that way. But it has been served to me many times at other people's homes from one large serving bowl, and it was fine.)

Cover tightly with aluminum foil and refrigerate for 3 to 6 hours. (The mousse may stand longer—12 to 24 hours if you wish. The texture will become more spongy and less creamy. Delicious both ways.)

MOCHA CREAM

1 cup heavy cream
¼ cup confectioners sugar
1 tablespoon instant coffee

In a chilled bowl with chilled beaters, beat the above ingredients only until the cream thickens to the consistency of a heavy custard sauce—not stiff.

Pour or spoon the cream onto the mousse to completely cover the top of each portion.

Refrigerate until serving time.

(Reprinted with permission from Maida Heatter's Book of Great Chocolate Desserts, Alfred A. Knopf, 1978)

Maida Heatter

CARL HIAASEN

Columnist/ Author

This is my recipe for Key West Grouper Sandwich. It's not fancy , but nothing in all Florida tastes any better:

1. Go to Key West.
2. Get in a boat.
3. Ride out to one of the patch reefs off Woman Key.
4. Using a small chunk of cut balao on a medium-weight spinning rod, catch a grouper. Three pounds is the ideal weight.

5. Race back to Key West and find a place with a stove.

6. Carefully fillet the grouper, dip it in egg yolk, roll it in bread crumbs and lay it in a skillet to fry.

7. Quick, while the fish is frying, race out to the store and buy some thick Bahamian bread -- johnnycake is perfect. Now, race back to the kitchen.

8. Carefully take the fish out of the fry pan and lay the filets on the bread.

9. Open a cold beer. Wait for fish to cool for two minutes in order to avoid scalding your tongue to charred nub.

10. After sandwich has quit steaming, eat the sucker.

WARNING: This recipe won't work unless you catch the fish yourself, personally. If you try this with a Key West grouper that somebody else has caught, a large fishbone will lodge in your throat and you will make a big mess of lunch.

BROWARD COMMUNITY COLLEGE

OFFICE OF THE PRESIDENT

Because Cool Counts

Below are two warm weather favorites at our house that are easy to prepare and will help keep you cool.

GAZPACHO

1-1/2 cups tomato juice	2 tablespoons wine vinegar
1 beef bouillon cube	1 tablespoon salad oil
1 tomato, chopped	1/2 teaspoon salt
1 cucumber, chopped	1/2 teaspoon Worcestershire
1 green pepper, chopped	Sauce
1 onion, chopped	3 drops Tabasco

Dissolve bouillon cube in 1/4 cup water in microwave. Add to cold tomato juice. Stir in remaining ingredients; chill several hours. Serve with herbed croutons. This receipe will serve approximately five people when served as an appetizer. In our family, we triple the recipe and keep the remainder, if any, for a snack.

BULGUR SALAD

2 cups water
1 cup bulgur (cracked wheat) - get this in bulk at health
   food store
1 cucumber, pared and cubed
1 tomato, cubed
1 green bell pepper, cubed
1 bunch green onions, trimmed and cut into 1/4" slices
1/4 cup parsley, finely chopped
2 teaspoons salt
1/2 teaspoon pepper
3 tablespoons lemon juice
1/4 cup olive oil

Bring water to boil in two-quart saucepan and slowly pour in bulgur. Cover and simmer for ten minutes, or until all water has been absorbed. Uncover, and stirring frequently, cook over low heat for another few minutes to dry the grains. In large bowl cool to room temperature and then refrigerate at least 30 minutes, until thoroughly chilled. (Bulgur may be somewhat sticky - don't worry - grains will separate when oil and lemon juice are added.) Add vegetables to chilled bulgur. Season. Sprinkle in lemon juice and olive oil. Toss salad lightly but thoroughly making sure to separate grains of bulgur. Chill until ready to serve. (Serves four generously.)

Will Holcombe

Willis N. Holcombe

The Miami Herald

A KNIGHT-RIDDER NEWSPAPER

THE MIAMI HERALD PUBLISHING CO. • 1 HERALD PLAZA, MIAMI, FLORIDA 33101 • (AREA CODE 305) 350-2111

Cornbread Dressing
a la Anna Stahr Hosmon
as told to her son, Robert Stahr Hosmon

I have great memories of my childhood in Mississippi, and one of the great taste treats of that childhood was my mother's cornbread dressing. I still like it best when she makes it, but when I get nostalgic--and hungry--her recipe helps me to relive those childhood memories.

The recipe begins with the cornbread itself, prepared by mixing in a bowl one cup of self-rising corn meal, one cup of buttermilk, one egg, and pinch of salt. In a cast iron skillet melt two tablespoons of bacon grease and coat the bottom and the sides of the skillet with the melted fat. Pour any excess grease into the meal mixture and blend. Then pour the entire meal mixture into the hot skillet and place the skillet in a 450 degree oven. Bake until the top of the cornbread is a golden brown and the sides of the bread easily pull away from the skillet.

To continue with the dressing, crumble half of the cornbread together with eight slices of stale white bread into a large bowl. Add three large tablespoons of poultry seasoning, one and a half teaspoons of salt, a dash of black pepper. one whole egg and four cups of chicken broth (adding the broth one cup at a time, while stirring). Transfer to a suitable baking dish and bake at 425 degrees until the top of the dressing is light brown. Serve hot with chicken or turkey, and a bottle of chilled Monterey Vineyards White Zinfandel.

Bob Hosmon
Wine Editor

Hot·Jazz & Alligator·Gumbo·Society, Inc.

1048 S.W. 49th Terrace
Plantation, FL 33317
(305) 581-4310

A Non-profit Society Devoted to the Perpetuation, Advancement and Performance of Heritage Jazz

The above material, of Obscure Origin, was discovered in the Archives of the Hot Jazz & Alligator Gumbo Society and may be the sole Authoritative recipe for the concoction. It is reproduced here as a service to Members, Friends and Others who are interested in haute cuisine.

Patti Phipps Houston

FRESH STRAWBERRY OMELET WITH SOUR CREAM

Sweeten sliced fresh strawberries to taste. If you wish, add 1/4 teaspoon sugar per egg before mixing omelet. Fill omelet with 2 teaspoons strawberries for each egg used. Fold and top with dollops of sour cream, dust with powered sugar, and pass under a hot broiler just long enough to set sour cream. Garnish with whole strawberries!!

Patti Phipps Houston

A few years ago, a fisherman discovered the broadbill swordfish in large numbers off the South Florida coast. In short order, swordfish steaks became popular at local fish markets and restaurants. But whether broiled over coals or baked in the oven, some folks found the fish rather dry and grainy table fare.

Here's a cooking tip and recipe concocted by my Mom in Cape Cod, where fresh swordfish steaks are a tradition at New Bedford markets and throughout coastal New England. Mom's trick keeps swordfish really moist without disguising the fish's delicate flavor.

                    SWORDFISH ALA MAGGIE

Fresh Swordfish steaks (1-inch thick)
Fresh or dryed dill weed seasoning
Black pepper
Fresh squeezed lemon juice
Mayonnaise

Cover the fish liberally with mayonnaise. Add pepper, dill, and squeeze on lemon juice before and during cooking. Bake in a shallow dish at 300-350 degrees until topping is lightly browned and bubbling and the fish flakes with a fork.

Best served with broiled tomato halves with parsley, fresh peas and celery to add color and texture to the entree.

                              Enjoy,

                              Roger Hurlburt

                              Arts/Entertainment Writer

Ryder System, Inc.
3600 NW 82 Avenue
Miami, Florida 33166
305 593-3695

Edwin A. Huston
Senior Executive Vice President-Finance

RYDER SYSTEM

LINGUINE ALLA CECCA

5 large tomatoes, peeled, seeded & chopped
1 cup chopped fresh basil leaves
1/2 cup extra virgin olive oil
2 cloves garlic, crushed
Hot red pepper flakes to taste (1/2 - 1 tsp.)
Salt to taste (1/2 - 1 tsp.)
1 lb. linguine

Combine ingredients, except pasta, and let stand
at room temperature several hours. Cook linguine.
Serve sauce over hot pasta. Pass parmesan cheese.

Variations:

> Substitute angel hair for linguine.
> Add cubed mozarella and/or sliced black olives.

This is a light, refreshing pasta, especially in
the summer when fresh basil and tomatoes are
abundant.

Serves 4.

Ed & Jane Huston

JOHN HUTCHINSON ....."HUTCH".

6pm - 10pm weeknights... also Research Director.

A good meal starts with a good cocktail! Try these on for size!

"THE VULCAN MIND PROBE"

OUZO over ice...pour 151 RUM over it.....watch it melt !! Defies all logic !!

THE '57 T'BIRD WITH HAWAIIAN PLATES

VODKA
GRAND MARNIER
SOUTHERN COMFORT
TRIPLE SEC
SWEET AND SOUR
GRENADINE
PINEAPPLE JUICE

A shot of each mixed over ice...
strain into shot glasses.
Watch your guests try to find their cutlery !!

"THE SCREAMING WHITE PUERTO RICAN PANEL TRUCK"

MYERS 151
MYERS DARK
CREAM O'COCONUT
KALUAH
CREAM

Good even for dessert!!!!

To FOLLOW.....

TERIYAKI DOLPHIN

CUT DOLPHIN STEAKS AS DESIRED.
PLACE IN LARGE SHALLOW DISH.
SPRINKLE WITH CRUSHED PEPPERS.
COVER WITH ABOUT 1/4 CUP OF
WORCESTERSHIRE SAUCE.
SPRINKLE A LITTLE CAYENNE OR WHITE
PEPPER OVER THE DOLPHIN.
ADD TERIYAKI SAUCE WITHOUT DISTURBING
THE TOPPINGS, SO THAT THE FISH IS JUST
VISIBLE.
MARINATE FOR ONE OR TWO HOURS, TURNING THE FISH
OVER ABOUT EVERY THIRTY MINUTES.
SMOKE THE DOLPHIN IN A KETTLE TYPE GRILL AND
BASTE WITH THE MARINADE SAUCE.
CURRY POWDER, CUMIN OR PAPRIKA CAN BE ADDED
TO THE MARINADE FOR BASTING FOR A VARIATION
IN TASTE..... BUT ONLY LIGHTLY.

HUTCH'S WING SAUCE

PREPARE......
2 BOTTLES DURKEES HOT SAUCE
1 JAR DURKEES MUSTARD MAYONNAISSE.
(If latter not available, mix 1 jar
of Dijon Poupon with about 2 cups
Mayo.)
ADD TWO TABLESPOONS OF HORSERADISH .
STIR IN ABOUT SIX GOOD SHAKES OF
WORCESTERSHIRE SAUCE.

IN A SUITABLE PAN.......

MELT 1 STICK OF BUTTER
AND TAKE OFF SCUM WITH WOODEN
SPOON.
ADD HOT SAUCE MIXTURE TO PAN
AND STIR OVER LOW HEAT UNTIL
ALL IS OF ONE CONSISTENCY.

PREPARE AND DEEP FRY WINGS..IF YOU
HAVE A WOK... USE IT FOR LESS GREASE!
PLACE COOKED WINGS IN A SEPARATE PAN
POUR SAUCE OVER WINGS OVER LOW HEAT
AND STIR AROUND UNTIL COVERED.

Bon Appetit ! Hutch

Gilmore Broadcasting Corporation

There is something inherently funny in asking me to provide a recipe for a celebrity cookbook. First of all, the semi-loyal readers of my column in the Miami Herald's Broward edition would question my celebrity, and my lovely new wife Dorothy would question my qualifications as a chef.

Actually I'm a pretty good cook within the narrow definition of the word. I simply take whatever meat or seafood I can find in the refrigerator and cook it in a lot of garlic or wine. Very chic. Never once have I written down what I used.

So this recipe started with my buddy, Scott. He provided the ingredients, then hung up the phone before explaining what to do with them. I remembered a few tricks my Dad showed me around the old backyard grill, then asked my friend, Herald food writer Lucy Cooper, for her suggestions. And you know what? I think it tastes great.

COUNT BASIL BBQ CHICKEN

Make a marinade from:
- 4 oz. vermouth
- 4 oz. gin
- 4 oz. virgin olive oil
- 2 oz. lime juice
- 2 tablespoons sweet basil
- 2 tablespoons thyme
- 2 cloves garlic (not crushed)

Marinate eight pieces of fresh chicken breast with the bones in (Lucy says this keeps the meat moist). Let the chicken soak for at least an hour, but overnight is best.

Prepare your fire, spreading the coals evenly along the bottom of the grill and setting the grate at about medium height. Once the coals are white hot, cook for about five minutes on each side, starting with the bone side down. Baste the chicken liberally with the remaining marinade sauce as you go, but watch for flare-ups from the fire.

Some of the leftover marinade can be used to saute fresh mushrooms in a skillet on the stove. I also spread it on the French bread before sprinkling parmesan cheese on top and broiling in the oven.

Serve chicken on a platter with wedges of lime. Or perhaps, in keeping with the marinade, you'll want to adorn each piece with a martini olive on a toothpick.

Ron Ishoy

SALMON CASA VECCHIA

4 pieces fresh, center cut salmon fillet (8 ounces each)
2 medium leeks
2 medium carrots
8 fresh basil leaves
2 shallots (finely chopped)
1 cup good dry white wine
1 cup fish stock
¼ cup olive oil
½ cup butter
salt and fresh ground pepper

Clean and cut carrots, leeks and basil in small julienne strips.

In a skillet, melt one tablespoon of butter and olive oil on
high heat, add the shallots (finely chopped), leeks, carrots and
basil. Saute for two minutes, remove from the heat and keep
on the side.

Flour the salmon fillets on both sides. In a large skillet, on
medium heat, melt the butter. When the foaming subsides arrange
the fillets in the pan. Season them with salt and fresh ground
pepper. Lightly brown one side (about two minutes) then flip the
fillets over, season again, add the vegetables, wine and the fish
stock. After bringing to a boil, reduce the heat, simmer for
five minutes.

Place the fillets on warm plates with the vegetables on top of
the fish. Reduce the juices to half. When ready to serve, pour
over the salmon and serve with garnish of parsley and lemon
wedges on the side.

Henri Janneau
Chef

Red Snapper Fort Lauderdale

- 6 fillets of red snapper
- 12 orange sections
- 12 grapefruit sections
- 4 cups of mayonnaise
- 1/3 cup whipping cream
- 1/3 cup orange juice
- nutmeg - salt - pepper

Line a shallow baking dish, or pan, with foil, skin side down. Salt and pepper to taste.

Place an orange section and a grapefruit section on each fillet.

Combine the orange juice, mayonnaise, and cream. Beat until thick. (This prevents the mayonnaise from thinning out in the oven.)

Spread over fish. Sprinkle with nutmeg.

Bake in a 350° oven until fish flakes. About 8-12 minutes. Serves six. Garnish with dill and orange slices

If you wish to, serve with rice mixed with chopped pecans — OR rice and chopped dill with a few peas and red pepper slices, added to the rice.

Joanne Johnsen

Recipe from Coach Jimmy Johnson

Keys Conch Chowder

2 lbs. conch meat
3 cups chicken broth
2 large onions
2 cloves garlic
1 green pepper
1 red pepper
2 tablespoons butter
8 ounces tomato sauce
6 ounces tomato paste
3 medium potatoes, diced
1 teaspoon oregano
    salt & pepper to taste
    dash of hot pepper sauce
¼ cup sherry

Put conch through a food grinder, or process to small chunks in a food processor. Do not process to pulp. Or, pound conch with a mallet to tenderize and cut into small pieces. Cover with chicken broth and simmer for 30 minutes. Cut onions, garlic and peppers into dice. Saute in the butter until limp. Add to the conch and broth along with tomato sauce, tomato paste, potatoes, oregano and salt and pepper.

Simmer until potatoes are tender, about 30 minutes. Add hot pepper sauce and sherry, and simmer 5 minutes. Makes 8 servings.

Jimmy Johnson

FROM

SENATOR
    HARRY A. JOHNSTON II
    WEST PALM BEACH

APPLE-ORANGE COBBLER

5 COOKING APPLES

1/2 C FRESH ORANGE JUICE -
                        GRATE RINE

3/4 C SUGAR

        BUTTER

PEAL + SLICE 5 GOOD SIZE
APPLES INTO A CASSEROLE DISH
COVER WITH ORANGE JUICE,
RINE AND SUGAR. DOT WITH
BUTTER. PLACE SINGLE PIE CRUST
RIGHT ON TOP OF APPLES.

BAKE 350° OVEN FOR 30 MIN,

GRILLED DOLPHIN STEAK'ONION MARMALADE AND TOMATO BUTTER

Ingredients for 6 pers
5 lbs of fresh dolphin in filet
3 large yellow spanish onions peeled and sliced
10 big ripe tomatoes in quartered
1lbs of unsalted butter
3 T spoon of grenadine
6 T spoon of wine vinegar(best is balsamic vinegar)
2 garlic cloves
1 sprig of thyme
3 T spoon of olive oil
1 bunch of fresh basil

Prepare the onion marmalade

In a large sautepan,saute the onions with 1|3 of the butter,
stir occasionally to prevent the onions from browning(they should
be however completely soft)be patient this can be take up to 20 mn.Add
the grenadine,vinegar and salt keep the onion marmalade warm while
preparing the rest of the dish

Prepare the tomato butter

In a saucepan saute the quartered tomatoes in olive oil add the garlic
cloves,the thyme and the basil(guard 6 beautiful basil leaves for
the garnish).Cook for 10 mn over a medium flame,stiring once or twice.Put
all in a blender jar and while machine is running,add the butter
bit by bit.Strain into a saucepan taste for salt and keep warm but
do not reboil

To cook the fish

Salt and pepper both side of the dolphin steak.Oil lightly the surfaces
of the fish.Grill the dolphin on the barbecue or on a nonstick pan
on the stove

To serve

Serve on a bed of onion marmalade with the tomato butter around the
plate.Place the fish on the onion marmalade.Garnish with fresh basil.

ALAIN JORAND

The Harbour/ 2401 PGA Boulevard, Palm Beach Gardens, Florida 33410 / Tel: (305) 627-5994

JAMES JUDD
MUSIC DIRECTOR

JOSEPH LEAVITT
EXECUTIVE VICE PRESIDENT

RALPH A. MARRINSON
CHAIRMAN, BOARD OF GOVERNORS

LONDON LAMB ROAST

2 lb. best end or loin of lamb

Salt, white pepper, ginger

Mint jelly

Pre-heat oven to 400° F. Rub meat with salt, pepper and teaspoon of ginger.

Place on rack in tin and roast for 20 minutes. Prepare glazing of 1/2 cup mint jelly melted in 1/2 cup hot water. Continue to baste meat often for another 40 minutes until roasting completed. Lamb should be "pink".

Decorate roast with fresh mint leaves and thin slices of lemon. Serve with mint jelly.

James Judd
Music Director

EXECUTIVE OFFICES
1430 NORTH FEDERAL HIGHWAY, FT. LAUDERDALE, FL 33304-1494
BROWARD: (305) 561-2997   DADE: (305) 945-5180   BOCA RATON: (305) 392-5443   PALM BEACH: (305) 659-0331
BOCA RATON OFFICE
500 EAST SPANISH RIVER BOULEVARD, SUITE 27, BOCA RATON, FL 33431
(305) 392-7230

JAMES H. KIMBERLY

POST OFFICE BOX 351
PALM BEACH, FLORIDA 33480
(305) 655-1844

One of my favorite recipes is, "Caneton A La Presse",
or pressed duckling. These do not have to be wild ducks.
I believe, farm-raised Mallard can be equally good. The
rest of the recipe is quite simple. The only thing that
is required is a duck press. These are not easy to find
but are necessary for this recipe:

"Rub young, wild ducklings inside and out with
brandy or lemon juice mixed with salt and pepper.
Roast ducks for 18-20 minutes at 425° (underdone).
Place the birds on a heated platter, cover them
with a hood and bring to the table, where a duck
press and hot chafing dish are ready.

In the chafing dish, place 2 tablespoons of butter
and saute in it a tablespoon of chopped shallots;
add a tablespoon of currant jelly and simmer for
about 3 minutes. Add 2 ounces of cognac and a
half cup of dry, red wine. Simmer...

Meanwhile, carve off the breasts with a sharp
knife. The thigh and legs can go back to the
kitchen for a few more minutes of cooking and
then be cut up to be served with the breast.

Break the duck carcases and put in well of the
press. Turn the pressure wheel and force the
blood through the press into a heated dish. Add
this to the sauce, along with the carved breasts and
the juice drained from the ducklings during carving.
Baste the breast meat with the sauce and when all
is well heated, serve at once on very hot plates with
wild rice."

Good Luck!
Jim Kimberly

87

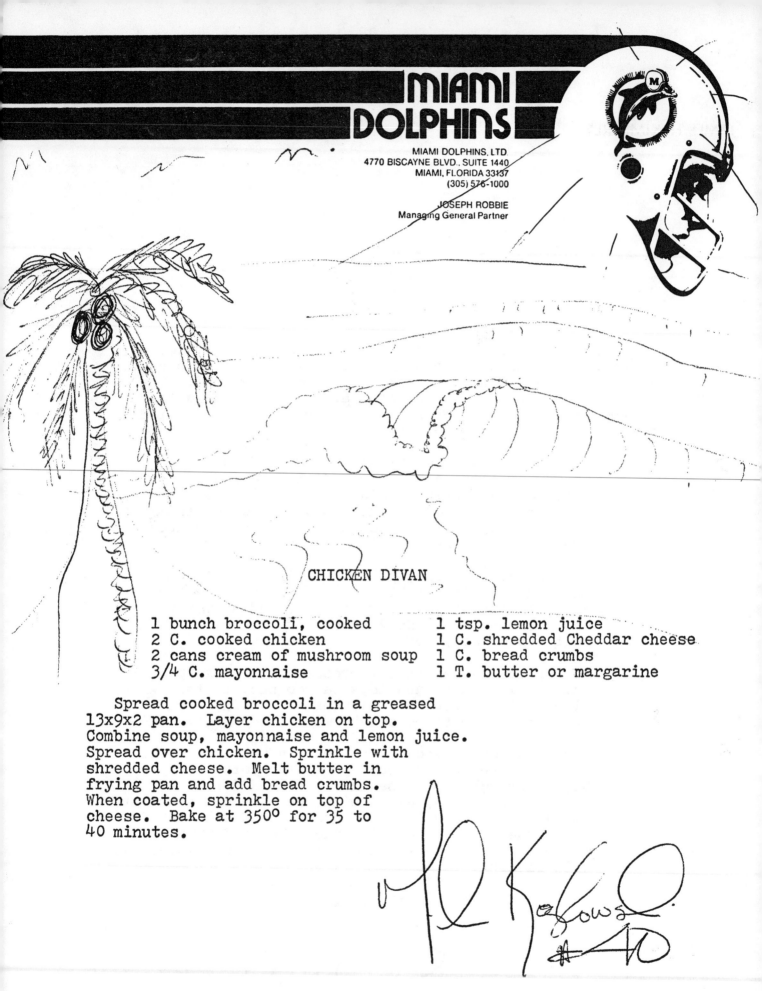

MIAMI DOLPHINS

MIAMI DOLPHINS, LTD
4770 BISCAYNE BLVD., SUITE 1440
MIAMI, FLORIDA 33137
(305) 576-1000

JOSEPH ROBBIE
Managing General Partner

CHICKEN DIVAN

1 bunch broccoli, cooked	1 tsp. lemon juice
2 C. cooked chicken	1 C. shredded Cheddar cheese
2 cans cream of mushroom soup	1 C. bread crumbs
3/4 C. mayonnaise	1 T. butter or margarine

Spread cooked broccoli in a greased
13x9x2 pan. Layer chicken on top.
Combine soup, mayonnaise and lemon juice.
Spread over chicken. Sprinkle with
shredded cheese. Melt butter in
frying pan and add bread crumbs.
When coated, sprinkle on top of
cheese. Bake at 350° for 35 to
40 minutes.

Bahamian Snapper
created by Chef Martin Kratish

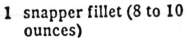

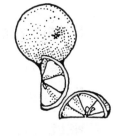

- 1 snapper fillet (8 to 10 ounces)
- ½ cup all-purpose flour
- 2 eggs, lightly beaten
- 4 tablespoons clarified butter
- 2 ounces Tropical Rum
- 1 ounce orange curacao
- Juice of ½ orange
- 2 tablespoons toasted sliced almonds
- 4 ounces fish stock, thickened with 1 tablespoon cornstarch
- 3 ounces pina colada mix
- 2 slices kiwi fruit
- 1 strawberry
- 1 banana, cut in half lengthwise

Heat saute pan to smoking point. While pan is heating, dredge snapper in flour, then egg. Add clarified butter to pan and saute fish on both sides until it turns a light golden brown. Add rum, orange juice, curacao, thickened fish stock, pina colada mix and toasted almonds. Cook over medium heat for 5 to 7 minutes until sauce thickens.

While fish is cooking, in a separate pan, saute banana in a small amount of clarified butter until golden brown. Place fish on platter, spooning sauce over it. Garnish with strawberry, kiwi and banana. Serves 1.

89

PLUM BOMBS A LA FOOTY

PREPARE AND CHILL WELL:

    ROLLED COOKIE DOUGH

PREPARE OVEN TO 350 DEGREES

DRAIN THOROUGHLY AND REMOVE PITS FROM:

    CANNED PLUMS

STUFF THEM WITH A COMBINATION OF:

    PINE NUTS AND WHITE RAISINS OR CHOPPED LARGER NUTS

ENCLOSE THE PLUMS IN THIN WRAPPINGS OF THE ROLLED DOUGH. PLACE WELL APART ON A GREASED BAKING SHEET AND BAKE ABOUT 25 MINUTES OR UNTIL SLIGHTLY COLORED.

FROM "ATHLETE'S FOOT".....AKA.....JOHN KROSS, SPORTS DIRECTOR

2741 N. 29th Avenue • Suite 300 • Hollywood, Florida 33020 • Dade (305) 944-1956 • Broward (305) 925-7117 • Palm Beach (305) 655-0994

La Vieille Maison

SALAD DE CHAMPIGNONS

Serves Four

INGREDIENTS:

1 pound fresh white, firm mushrooms; best grade
1 cup vinaigrette dressing
3 oz. parmesan dressing
2 tablespoons chopped parsley
Boston or Butter lettuce preferred
(other lettuce may be substituted)

METHOD:

Wash mushrooms rapidly under cold running water. Slice
1/8" pieces. Cut parmesan cheese into very thin slices
(julienne), and dice crosswise. Toss mushrooms with the
vinaigrette dressing, parmesan cheese, and half of the
parsley. Arrange a thin bed of lettuce on previously
chilled plates, and mound with the remaining mixture.
Sprinkle with the remaining parsley.

VINAIGRETTE DRESSING

3 tablespoons red wine vinegar
1 tablespoon French Mustard (Dijon style)
3 tablespoons vegetable oil
Salt and white pepper to taste

Yves Labbe

Mrs. Silvia W. Leiferman

SWORDFISH WITH RED PEPPER SAUCE

Serves four

Marinate swordfish for two hours in juice of four lemons
and two limes. Sprinkle with ½ teaspoon cayenne pepper,
1 teaspoon of basil, ½ teaspoon dried tarragon, 1 teaspoon
rosemary, ¼ teaspoon of thyme, and 1 tablespoon of fresh
chopped parsley.

Grill fish over mesquite.

For red pepper sauce, these are the ingredients:

4 large red bell peppers
1½ cups of white wine
½ cup plain yogurt
2 teaspoons of lime juice

Half and seed peppers, and roast under broiler until they
are charred. Peel off skin and puree peppers in a blender
with ½ teaspoon white pepper.

In a quart saucepan, over medium high heat, reduce lime
juice in white wine to ¼ of a cup. Remove from heat and whisk
in yogurt, then add red pepper puree.

Cook fresh angle hair and spinach pasta in boiling salted
water. Pour equal amounts of red pepper sauce on four
plates, and coat. Make a nest on the sauce with the pasta,
and place grilled swordfish on the plate. Garnish with a
twisted lemon.

Mrs. Arvin H (Silvia) Leiferman

Mrs. Sylvia Leiferman

ORIOLE HOMES CORP.

1151 N.W. 24th Street - Pompano Beach, Florida 33064
Telephone (305) 972-7660   TWX: 510-956-9668

RICHARD D. LEVY
Chairman of the Board

JEWISH PIZZA

1 piece matzoh
2 slices muenster cheese

Lay the cheese on the matzoh. Heat in microwave
oven on high for 18 to 30 seconds, depending on
the intensity of the oven. Serve this luncheon
favorite with soda, lemonade or a milk shake.

Note: This recipe has not been patented.

Richard D. Levy

Roast Beef a la Captain

Choose a wrapped roast sirloin of beef...the kind with those
little pieces of string holding it together.
Take a clove of garlic and peel all the individual pieces.
If they are large cut them to the size of pencil erasers.
Next take small knife and make holes in the roast by stabbing it.
Take the peeled pieces of garlic and put them in the holes.
Cover the out side with a heavy coat of seasoned salt and garlic
powder. Pour worchester sauce into the holes after the garlic.
Pre-heat your oven to 375. Cook it until you suddenly smell the
aroma filling the room. Slice thin and sprinkle with garlic
powder as you slice. Slice the whole thing..it makes better
sandwiches the next day that way....

Mark "Captain X" Lipof
Producer, Sonny in the Morning Show

2741 N. 29th Avenue • Suite 300 • Hollywood, Florida 33020 • Dade (305) 944-1956 • Broward (305) 925-7117 • Palm Beach (305) 655-0994

Neiman-Marcus

FLORIDA VEAL LIMONE

Yield 4-6 servings

1 to 2 lemons, peeled, sliced into thin cartwheels
1½ lbs. Veal Steak ¼" thick
Salt and Pepper
Flour
2-4 tablespoons Oil (I use half butter-half oil)
1 cup Chicken Stock/Bouillon
½ teaspoon tarragon, crushed
1 teaspoon grated lemon peel
1 teaspoon freshly squeezed lemon juice
4 tablespoons water
Finely Snipped Fresh Parsley

Prepare lemon cartwheels, reserve. Cut veal into serving
pieces, score edges to prevent curling. Season with
salt and pepper; coat with flour. Saute a few at a time
in hot oil until nicely browned on both sides. Remove
from pan, drain off all but one tablespoon pan drippings.
Add chicken stock, tarragon, lemon peel and lemon juice.
Bring to a boil, scraping drippings loose from bottom
of pan. Add browned cutlets; simmer very gently for five
minutes or until tender. Remove to warm serving platter.
Add water to reduced drippings, stirring until smooth.
Should be thin, but not watery. Add reserved lemon
slices and heat a few seconds. Top each serving with one
or two lemon slices, cover with sauce, top with snipped
parsley. Excellent accompanied with Rice Pilaff.

2442 East Sunrise Boulevard
Ft. Lauderdale, Florida 33304
305 566 6666

This Recipe is for those who are willing to try the exotic taste of the Far East culinary marvel.

Ingredients: a dozen chicken livers (~ ½ lb), 2 gloves of minced fresh garlic, ½ tsp of crushed cumin seed, bunch of fresh basil leaves (or ½ tsp of dry basil), dry red pepper (to taste), 1 Tbsp of fish sauce (Vietnamese type), 1 tsp of sugar, 3 Tbsp of oil.

Heat oil on a skillet, add: garlic, red pepper, basil, fish sauce, sugar, cumin seed → bring them to sizzling hot. Add livers, stir fry for 3 to 5 minutes. Don't over cook the livers !!!

There, you have a wonderful dinner entrée, accompanied by stir-fry vegetables and steamed rice. For those who hate livers, substitute with minced chicken breast.

Bon appétit, mes amis et amies!

Tan Ly

Florida House of Representatives

Anne Mackenzie
Representative, 95th District

Committees

Joint Committee on Information
 Technology Resources, Chair
Governmental Operations, Vice Chair
Finance & Taxation
Criminal Justice
Regulated Industries & Licensing

LAMB SHISH KEBOB

1 small leg of lamb
16-20 small onions
10-20 small potatoes
32 large mushroom caps
4 green peppers
cherry tomatoes

Have lamb cut into 1 1/2" squares. Marinade overnight in marinade using red wine. Parboil potatoes and onions until barely tender. Thread meat and vegetables on long skewers in this order: mushroom, green pepper, potatoes, onion, green peppers and mushrooms. Allow 4-5 pieces of lamb, 2-3 potatoes, 2-3 onions, 2 green peppers and 4 mushrooms per person. Cook over coals turning frequently and brushing meat with the remaining marinade.

MARINADE

1 cup red dry wine
2 tablespoons wine vinegar
1/2 cup salad oil
1 clove crushed garlic
1 large grated onion
thyme
marjoram
cayenne pepper
2 teaspoons salt

Marinade and baste 4-6 hours

Anne

Reply to:
☐ Suite 105
  1000 South Federal Highway
  Fort Lauderdale, FL
  33316
  (305) 524-1000

☐ 308 House Office Building
  Tallahassee, FL
  32399-1300
  (904) 488-0245

California Caesar Salad

Leave 1 clove garlic, peeled and sliced in
½ cup olive oil, none other, for 24 hours.

Saute 1 cup cubed French Bread in 2 tablespoons
of the garlic & olive oil.

Break up into 2-inch lengths 2 heads romaine.
Wash in real cold water and dry well. Place
the romaine in a salad bowl.

Sprinkle over it:
   ~~1½ teaspoons salt~~
   ¼ teaspoon dry mustard
   A generous grating of black pepper
   5 fillets of anchovy, cut up small or
      mashed to a paste
   A few drops of Worcestershire sauce

Add:
   3 tablespoons wine vinegar and the
   remaining 6 tablespoons garlic oil.

Drop 1 egg from the shell onto the ingredients
in the bowl. Squeeze over the egg the juice
of 1 lemon.

Add the croutons, 2 to 3 tablespoons Parmesan
cheese, and small chunks of Blue cheese.

Toss the salad well. Serve it at once. Serves 4.

Ralph A. Marrinson

FLORIDA ORANGE COCONUT MERINGUE PIE

1 Cup Orange Juice
1 Cup Orange sections, cut in pieces
2 Tablespoons grated, Orange rind
1 Cup sugar
5 Tablespoons cornstarch
3 Egg yolks, beaten
2 Tablespoons butter or margarine
2 Tablespoons lemon juice
  Enough coconut to sprinkle lightly over
  meringue

Combine orange juice, sections, grated rind,
sugar and cornstarch. Cook on low heat until
clear. Add a little hot mixture to beaten egg
yolks. Cook about 5 minutes longer. Remove
from heat. Blend in lemon juice, butter or
margarine. Pour into baked pie shell. Be sure
filling and shell are both hot or both cold.
Cover filling with meringue. Sprinkle with
coconut. Bake in 350° oven until lightly
browned.

Bob Martinez

IRRESISTIBLES

Kitchen Shop and School by Debbie Mastriana

SEAFOOD COQUILLE

12 tablespoons butter, divided
6 tablespoons flour
2 teaspoons salt
¼ teaspoon white pepper
4 cups light cream
1 pound scallops, soaked in milk at least 30 min. - drain well
½ cup finely chopped onion
1 cup sliced mushrooms
1 pound cooked shrimp
½ pound crabmeat or lobster, cleaned well
¼ cup sherry
6 tablespoons fine bread crumbs
Pimiento

Melt 9 tablespoons butter in a saucepan; blend flour in smoothly and cook the roux over low heat for several minutes, stirring frequently. Season roux with salt and white pepper; Gradually stir in light cream, and cook sauce, stirring constantly until it begins to bubble. Simmer it over low heat for 5 minutes.

In a skillet, saute scallops and onions in 3 tablespoons butter until the onions are golden. Remove the scallops and onions and in the same skillet saute the sliced mushrooms for 3 minutes. Combine the mushrooms with the scallops, onions, and cream sauce. Stir in the shrimp, crabmeat, and sherry.

Spoon the mixture into a casserole or individual scallop shells and sprinkle with bread crumbs. Bake the coquille at 400 degrees for 10 minutes or until bread crumbs are slightly browned. Garnish the dish with bits of pimiento and serve at once as a first course or an entree.

Serves 10 to 12 - first course

IT'S IRRESISTIBLE!

Debbie S Mastriana

4215 North Federal Highway
Ft. Lauderdale, Florida 33308
(305) 564-8884

 **MIAMI-DADE**
COMMUNITY COLLEGE

Robert H. McCabe
President

Number one in America.

Potato Pancakes

Forget this one if you are on a diet.

While my name is Irish, most of my family have German backgrounds and my potato pancakes recipe is from my mother's family, the Greers. My wife, Bonnie, is a splendid southern style cook and this is one of the few items that gets me entry into the kitchen.

Potato pancakes <u>must</u> be served hot - in our family Bonnie and I take turns cooking and the pancakes are served right from the pan. Applesauce is the traditional side dish.

Some years ago I learned from my Jewish friend, Jack Skigen, that matza meal is better than flour in the recipe and I made that change, but flour does work.

<u>Ingredients:</u>   5 very large baking potatoes
                   or an equivalent amount of smaller potatoes
                2 medium onions
                1 tablespoon of salt, or to taste
                2 eggs
                1 teaspoon of baking powder
                   sufficient matza meal to absorb liquid

<u>Steps:</u>   1. Grate potatoes and squeeze as dry as possible in a close gauge strainer.
        2. Add grated onions, unbeaten eggs, salt and baking powder.
        3. Hand mix.
        4. Add sufficient matza meal to absorb liquid - in time you will recognize the right consistency, but typically it would be approximately 5 tablespoons.
        5. Hand mix.
        6. Heat oil to moderate heat in a pan.
        7. Spoon in pancake mix with a large tablespoon, then spread so that each pancake is approximately one-half inch thick. Fork turn when golden brown.
        8. Place on folded paper towels to absorb oil and serve immediately.
        9. As you use the mix it will often have more liquid. You can then add more matza meal.

Guten appetit !

Robert H. McCabe
President

Mayhue's
SUPER LIQUOR STORES
The Liquor Department Stores

CENTRAL OFFICE
625 NORTHEAST 4th STREET
FT. LAUDERDALE, FLORIDA 33301

"First Original Store — 1946"

Carl Mayhue

ROAST SUCKLING PIG

There are occasions when Suckling Pig is absolutely necessary for special gala parties, such as a luau. A recipe is most difficult to find.

This recipe for the old-fashioned way of cooking a young pig is given because it is pleasant to preserve traditional rules. However, there is no reason why you should not dress and season a pig and roast it throughout in a moderate oven 350°, allowing 30 to 35 minutes to the pound.

A SUCKLING PIG

Wash it well. Dry it inside and out. The dressed pig should weigh about 12 pounds. Rub the inside with:

1 TABLESPOON SALT

Fill the pig with:

DRESSING

Onion dressing is traditional, but choose your favorite kind. It takes 2½ quarts of dressing to stuff a pig of this size. Multiply all your ingredients but not the seasonings. Use these sparingly until the dressing is combined, then taste it and add what is lacking. Sew up the pig. Put a block of wood in the pig's mouth to hold it open. Skewer the legs into position, pulling the forelegs forward and the hindlegs backward. Rub the pig with:

A CUT CLOVE OF GARLIC (OPTIONAL)

SALT

OIL OR SOFT BUTTER

Dredge it with:

FLOUR

Cover the ears with pieces of well-greased paper. Secure them with paper clips. Place the pig in a pan in a hot oven 480° for 15 minutes. Reduce the heat to a moderate oven 350°. Roast the pig until it is tender, allow 30 minutes to the pound.

ROAST SUCKLING PIG
(continued)

If you wish the surface of the roast to be soft, baste it every 15 minutes with boiling:

STOCK OR STOCK SUBSTITUTE

If you wish the surface to be crusty, baste it every 15 minutes with:

OIL OR MELTED BUTTER

and dredge it with:

FLOUR

It may be sprinkled very lightly each time with:

SALT
PAPRIKA

Remove the paper from the ears for the last 30 minutes of baking. Place the roast on a platter. Remove the wood from the mouth. Replace it with a small:

LEMON, APPLE OR CARROT

Place in the eyes:

RAISINS OR CRANBERRIES

Place all around the neck a wreath of:

SMALL GREEN LEAVES

or garnish the platter with:

PARSLEY OR WATERCRESS

The pig may be surrounded with:

CINNAMON APPLES
APPLES FILLED WITH SWEET POTATOES
APPLES FILLED WITH MINCEMEAT
BAKED TOMATOES FILLED WITH PINEAPPLE
ETC.

Mary R. McCahill
CURRY FOR EIGHT

2 lbs veal or chicken cubed
2 medium onions chopped

Saute together until cooked. Stir constantly
with wooden spoon.
Add salt and pepper
1 chopped apple
2 chopped bananas
2 tablespoons chutney
1 dozen seeded grapes
1 tablespoon dried raisins
1 can chicken broth

Stir into this curry powder to taste.
Simmer gently one-half hour. Marinate over
night.

Serve with:

Grated fresh coconut
Pineapple - crushed or chunks
Mandarin orange segments
Chutney
Preserved kumquats
Candied ginger pieces
Chopped fresh tomatoes

Mary R McCahill

CHEESE WAFERS

One-half pound sharp cheddar cheese, finely grated
One and three-fourths cups all-purpose flour
One-eighth teaspoon cayenne pepper
One-eighth teaspoon salt
One and one-half sticks butter

Mix dry ingredients in large bowl. Add butter in small
bits and blend until mixture is like coarse crumbs. Add
grated cheese and blend with fingers or pastry blender.
Work until pastry is yellow all the way through. (Since
the Food Processor became a fixture in my kitchen, these
steps became so easy. The butter is cut in by quickly
turning the machine off and on. The grated cheese is added
a handful at the time until all of it is incorporated into the pastry.)

The pastry may be chilled, rolled to $\frac{1}{4}$ inch thickness
and cut into strips 2" x 1" for baking. Or, it may be formed
into long rolls about $1\frac{1}{4}$" in diameter and chilled and cut
into slices. These biscuits are usually topped with a pe-
can half before baking. My favorite is to put pastry in
a heavy cookie press, make into ribbons and cut into pieces
about 1" x 2". However you choose to form them, bake at
375 degrees on cookie sheets until they begin to brown
very lightly. Cool completely and store in air-tight container.

These are wonderful to serve with a glass of
wine. Also, they are good with a salad. They
freeze well if you can keep them long enough to get
them into your freezer! The recipe comes from
my native state of North Carolina and the wafers
were always served at any celebration in my
home there. They are considered to be a necessity
at holiday time by my family.

Anna McDaniel

LEG OF LAMB

1. Using 5 garlic cloves, make slits in top
   of lamb and stuff with garlic. Mark with
   toothpicks for easy removal.

2. Sprinkle with salt and pepper. Cover with
   Dijon mustard and sprinkle with parsley.

3. Cook at 325º. One half hour before finished,
   baste with half bottle of red burgundy wine.

4. When cooked, remove from liquid. Skim grease
   by putting liquid in plastic container. Freeze.
   Grease will rise to top and is easier to
   remove.

ENJOY!!!!

3000 WEST ALAMEDA AVENUE, BURBANK, CALIFORNIA, 91523

Congress of the United States
House of Representatives
Washington, DC 20515

June 20, 1987

ISLAND CHICKEN MARINADE

1 cup salad oil
1/3 cup lemon juice
3 tablespoons soy sauce
1 clove garlic, minced
1 teaspoon oregano
½ teaspoon salt
¼ teaspoon pepper
2 frying chickens, about
   2 lbs. each

Combine all ingredients except chicken. Pour over
cut up chicken and marinate for an hour or longer
if desired. May be oven broiled, baked, or charcoal
broiled. Enjoy!

DANIEL A. MICA, M.C. (D-Fla., 14th)

CALIFORNIA CUISINE & WINE BAR

WHOLE GRILLED FLORIDA SNAPPER WITH LIME, PEANUT, CHILI SAUCE

1½ lb. Florida Snapper (either Yellowtail or Hog Snapper)
scaled and trimmed.

Fish is brushed with sesame oil and seasoned with salt and pepper.
Fish is then grilled over hard wood fire (Mesquite, Orange Wood, Oak
or Apple) for 15 to 20 minutes. The last 4 or 5 minutes of cooking time
the sauce is brushed over the fish.

Peanut, Lime, Chili Sauce
Makes about 1 quart

Ingredients:

Peanuts (dry roasted unsalted)	6 ounces/dry weight
Peanut Oil	1 cup
Sesame Oil	¼ cup
Hot Sesame Oil	1/8 cup
Onion	1 - diced
Tomato	1 - diced
Chili (Oriental)	4 each
Honey	1 cup
Soy Sauce	1 cup
Cilantro	6 sprigs whole
Fish Stock	1 cup
Garlic	1 T
Ginger	1 T
Lime	Juice ½ Lime

Roast Peanuts and Reserve

In all three oils saute onion, tomato, chilis, garlic, ginger, add to
that liquid ingredients and nuts and cilantro. Puree to a coarse consistency.

Executive Chef
Mark Militello

Wildflower

551 East Palmetto Park Road
Boca Raton, Florida, 33432

Boca Raton
391-0000
Broward County
426-0066

Sweet and Sour Curry Dressing

1/2 cup salad oil
1/2 cup red wine vinegar
2/3 cup sugar
3 Tablespoons lemon juice
4 teaspoons chili sauce
1 teaspoon Worcestershire
1/2 teaspoon dry mustard
1/4 teaspoon curry powder
few dashes tabasco sauce
1 clove garlic, crushed

Combine - yield: 1-1/4 cups

Excellent in salads or as an accompaniment for meats, fish, or poultry.

Stanley
Miskovsky

THE SEAGRAM CLASSICS WINE COMPANY

5430 BAY CENTER DRIVE

TAMPA, FL 33609

(813) 872-7911

LEWIS MILLER
VICE PRESIDENT
SOUTHERN DIVISION MANAGER

LOBSTER & LINGUINI

2 - 1 1/4 lb. Lobsters (steam 12 minutes)

Break claw into one piece, take tail meat out of shell, put aside, covered with plastic.

Break off small legs and removing gills and eyes, save the body shell and tail shell. Chop coarsely the legs and shell.

2 - garlic cloves (mashed and chopped)
1 - medium leek (chop white and tender light green)
1 - tablespoon chopped parsley
1 - carrot - diced
  - pepper to taste (couple twists on a mill)

Glaze a large pan with olive oil, add chopped shells and above ingredients over medium high heat 8 to 10 minutes, shaking and turning in pan. Turn heat on high and add:

1 - cup The Monterey Classic White Wine. Boil until reduced to a couple tablespoons (very little liquid in pan). In about 6 minutes, add 1 bottle (8 oz.) of clam juice. Turn down heat and simmer covered about 10 minutes. Remove cover and cook another 5 minutes or so boiling liquid to about 3/4 cup. Strain, removing all solids and skim off any surface fat or film (use a little more wine if it gets too dry).

All of this can be done in advance, just bring the liquid and lobster back to room temperature.

If making fresh, in same pan, reheat reduced clam juice and wine sauce, add 1 cup of cream and reduce until it coats a spoon lightly.

Cut lobster tail into 4 or 5 medallions and put tail and claw meat into cream sauce over low heat to just heat through.

IMPORTED
MUMM CHAMPAGNES · BARTON & GUESTIER (B & G) · BROLIO · BERSANO
JULIUS KAYSER · DeMONTAL ARMAGNAC · CARMEL

CALIFORNIA
STERLING VINEYARDS · THE MONTEREY VINEYARD · BANDIERA WINERY

LOBSTER & LINGUINI (continued)

In a large pot, bring water to a boil, add salt and using
preferably fresh linguini (which cooks in a few seconds), cook
8 oz. (a package) and drain.

Add linguini to lobster and toss in the warm pan until it is
coated by the sauce. Serve on warm plates by putting linguini
in the center, the tail meat on top, the claws on the side, and
a tablespoon of red caviar (for texture over the tail meat).

Done in two stages, this really doesn't take long and with a
crisp green salad, it is a romantic and lovely dinner.

Serve The Monterey Vineyard Chardonnay with it or Mumm
Champagne if dinner is after the kids are in bed.

Lew Miller

Lew Miller

EXECUTIVE OFFICES

R. SCOTT MORRISON, JR.
PRESIDENT

Boca Raton

Hotel and Club

501 EAST CAMINO REAL
BOCA RATON, FLORIDA 33432-6127
AREA CODE 305 • 395-3000

LAMB AND WILD MUSHROOM STRUDEL WITH GARLIC AND ROSEMARY SAUCE
(4 PORTIONS)

3 OZ OLIVE OIL

1 LAMB RACK (NO FAT - TRIMMED, RESERVE BONES)

2 TBS DRY MORELS (SOAKED TO RECONSTITUTE IN WARM STOCK - SMALL DICED)

6 MEDIUM SHITTAKE MUSHROOMS (SMALL DICED)

4 DOMESTIC MUSHROOMS (SMALL DICED)

1/4 CUP ASST. WILD AVAILABLE MUSHROOMS

2 1/2 TBS FRESH ROSEMARY (MINCED)

2 TBS GARLIC (MINCED)

1 TBS SHALLOTS (MINCED)

6 SHEETS STRUDEL PHYLLO LEAVES

1/2 # MELTED BUTTER

1 PAINT BRUSH (NEW)

SALT AND PEPPER TO TASTE

(*NOTE, RESERVE JUICE FROM RECONSTITUTED MORELS AS WELL AS ALL
  TRIMMINGS FROM MUSHROOMS.)

4 OZ DRY SHERRY

2 OZ BRANDY

2 CUPS CHICKEN STOCK

1 TBS TOMATO PASTE

TO MAKE SAUCE:

ROAST RESERVED LAMB BONES WITH MUSHROOM SCRAPS AND TOMATO PASTE
IN OVEN TILL BROWN, REMOVE FROM OVEN, DRAIN OFF ANY FAT, PLACE PAN
ON STOVE TOP AND DEGLAZE WITH 2 OZ SHERRY AND 1 OZ BRANDY, BRING
TO A BOIL, ADD CHICKEN STOCK AND MUSHROOMS JUICE. SIMMER ADDING
GARLIC TRIMMINGS, STEMS FROM FRESH ROSEMARY AND ANY FLAVOR
ENHANCING TRIMMINGS (VEGETABLE TRIMMINGS). AFTER SIMMERING FOR
45 MINUTES STRAIN INTO A CLEAN SMALL POT AND RESERVE.

Boca Raton

HOTEL and CLUB

TO MAKE FILLING:

DICE LAMB RACK AND BROWN WELL IN OLIVE OIL IN A HEAVY GAUGE PAN.
ADD MUSHROOMS, ROSEMARY, GARLIC, SHALLOTS, SALT AND PEPPER,
STIR IN WELL WITH LAMB, REMOVE FILLING FROM PAN, AND RETURN PAN
TO STOVE, USING REMAINING LIQUOR (2 OZ. SHERRY, 1 OZ. BRANDY)
DEGLAZE PAN THEN ADD STRAINED STOCK AND SIMMER, MOISTEN LAMB
AND MUSHROOM FILLING WITH 2-3 TBSP OF LAMB SAUCE, SHOULD BE
AT GLAZE CONSISTENCY AND RESERVED FOR PLATING.

TO ROLL STRUDEL:

LAY OUT 1 STRUDEL LEAF CAREFULLY, AND BRUSH WITH MELTED BUTTER,
THEN PROCEED TO REPEAT THIS PROCESS TWICE MORE MAKING THREE
LAYERS, DIVIDE LAMB FILLING IN FOUR PARTS, CUT STRUDEL LEAVES
IN 1/2 CROSSWISE AND PLACE, 1/4 MIX ON EACH SIDE: ROLL THE STRUDEL
UP AND TUCK IN ENDS AS YOU ROLL, REPEAT THIS PROCESS ONCE MORE
MAKING A TOTAL OF 4 STRUDELS, PLACE THEM ON A SHEET PAN BRUSH
WITH BUTTER, AND BAKE AT 375°-400° TILL GOLDEN BROWN ABOUT
8 - 10 MINUTES, SLICE STRUDEL DIAGONALLY WITH A KNIFE AND ARRANGE
ON A PLATE WITH THE SAUCE UNDER THE STRUDEL. GARNISH WITH
LARGE MOREL AND ROSEMARY SPRIG.

RSM:jm

R. SCOTT MORRISON, JR.
PRESIDENT

NICK NAVARRO
SHERIFF
BROWARD COUNTY

NAVARRO'S PAELLA

1/4 cup Olive oil	1 pkg. Frozen Peas
1/2 lb. Hot Italian Sausage	4 Chicken Bouillon Cubes
1 Chicken - cut up	4 cups Hot Water
Salt/Pepper/Oregano - to taste	1 tsp. Saffron
1 - 1 lb. pkg. Converted Rice	1 - 1 lb. can Tomatoes -
1 Lg. Onion - chopped	chopped with juice
1 Green Pepper - chopped	1 - 1 lb. Lobster Tail (or 2
2 cloves Garlic - chopped	small ones - Frozen
	1 jar Pimiento - cut in strips
	12 Clams

In a large deep pan, heat the oil. Fry the whole sausages
until done and browned. Remove sausage.

Sprinkle chicken with salt, pepper, and oregano to taste.
Brown chicken in drippings. Remove chicken.

Add garlic, onion, green pepper and rice to the pan and
stir until rice is browned.

Dissolve bouillon cubes in hot water. Add to the rice mixture
along with the saffron, chicken, tomatoes, and sausage (which
has been cut in diagonal slices 1" thick). Cover tightly and
simmer 25 minutes, stirring occasionally.

With a sharp knife cut the frozen lobster tails, shell and
all, into 1" slices. Stir slices into paella. Add pimiento
strips and frozen peas. Cover and simmer 10 minutes.

Steam clams separately and place on top of mixture for garnish.

Serve from the pot.

Buen Apetito,

Nick Navarro

NICK NAVARRO
Sheriff of Broward County

2600 S.W. 4TH AVENUE / FT. LAUDERDALE, FL 33315 / 305-765-8900

●SWIM TEAM   JACK NELSON'S FISH CHOWDER

2 fish fillets
2 teaspoons salt
1 teaspoon thyme
3 bay leaves
3 spice leaves
1 teaspoon peppercorns
1 teaspoon ground cloves
4 tablespoons bacon fat
3 large onions, chopped
8 stalks celery, chopped
1 clove garlic, chopped
2 green peppers, chopped
1 pound 12-ounce tin tomatoes
10 ounce tin consomme
1 cup ketchup
8 sprigs parsley
2 tablespoons Worcestershire sauce
1/2 teaspoon curry powder
juice of 1 lemon
2 pounds potatoes
5 or 6 carrots
1/2 medium turnip
black rum, sherry and Gravey Master to taste
whole bunch of T.L.C.

Place fish heads and fillets in large kettle and cover with
water, then add next 6 ingredients. Bring to a boil and cook
till meat leaves the bones, about 15 minutes.
In large frying pan melt bacon fat and cook onions, celery,
garlic and green peppers till soft. Add next 7 ingredients
and simmer for 30 minutes. Peel and cut into bite size
pieces potatoes, carrots, and turnip. Par-boil in salted
water. Strain fish broth then remove fish from bones and
return meat, broth and spice leaves to kettle (no bones) .
Now add vegetables and their stock and stir in contents of
the frying pan. Salt to taste. Flavor with black rum,
sherry and Gravey Master to taste. Simmer gently for 3 1/2
hours, stirring occasionally. It makes about 20 servings.
It freezes well. Let your guests add drops of Sherry Peppers
to taste.

Enjoy! *Jack Nelson*

Confrérie de la Chaîne des Rôtisseurs

Bailliage de Fort Lauderdale

Le Premier Chapitre de la Floride

3471 North Federal Highway, Fort Lauderdale, Florida 33306

(305) 563-9000

GLEN KING PARKER
BAILLI

BAILLI HONORAIRE
LEES M. SCHADEL, JR., M.D.

SEA URCHIN CASSOULET L'ERMITAGE
Based on a dish conceived by
Chef du Cuisine Michael Blanchet
of L'Ermitage Restaurant in Los Angeles

3/4 lb. of white parts of leeks
1/2 lb. spinach
1/2 "tray" of sea urchin roe*
1/2 pt. warm heavy cream
1 bottle of fine California Chardonnay or white Burgundy
Fresh-cut chives

Julienne the leeks and cook in boiling water until thoroughly done. Wash the spinach and cook in boiling water until very well done. Keep both warm.

Discard any dark pieces of the sea urchin roe, place them in a small saucepan and barely cover with wine. Over a high heat, bring barely to a boil and immediately take off the fire. (It is better to undercook than overcook sea urchins.) Remove the sea urchins with a slotted spoon and place them in the cream to keep warm.

Boil down the remaining liquid until reduced by three-fourths. Off heat, add an equal amount of the cream. Add salt and white pepper to taste. Boil down this sauce until it is quite thick. (Optional: At this point, blend in 2 tablespoons of soft butter.)

Drain the spinach and leeks. Cover the bottoms of small, low cassoulet dishes with the spinach. Use a slotted spoon to place the sea urchins on top of the spinach. Cover the sea urchins with the leeks. Pour the sauce on top. Sprinkle with the chives.

Consume immediately with the balance of the wine. (This recipe serves 4 as an appetizer.)

* Sea urchin roe is available in small wooden trays at many Japanese sushi restaurants; for example, at "Nobi's" in Fort Lauderdale.

JERRY PATE ENTERPRISES, INC.

POST OFFICE BOX 1790
PENSACOLA, FLORIDA 32598-1790
(904) 932-3500

SOUTH OF THE BORDER LASAGNE

```
1   lb. ground beef
4   7" flour tortillas
2   (15oz.) cans tomato sauce
2   (1¼ oz.) package taco seasoning mix
1   (4 oz.) can chopped green chilles-drained and chopped
1   (6 oz.) can frozen avocado dip - thawed (optional)
1   cup (4oz.) shredded Monterey Jack cheese with jalapenos
1   cup velvetta cheese (or your favorite cheddar, etc.)
1   jalapeno pepper, sliced and seeded (optional)
```

Cook ground beef in a skillet until browned, stirring
to crumble. Drain well and set aside. Fry tortillas,
one at a time, in ¼" hot oil (375°) about 5 seconds on
each side, or until softened. Drain well on paper towels,
set aside. Combine tomato sauce and taco seasoning. Mix
in a medium saucepan, bring to a boil. Reduce heat and
simmer, uncovered for 10 min. Remove from heat. Reserve
one cup of mixture. Add beef and half of green chilles to
remaining sauce mixture.

Place a tortilla and half of meat mixture in greased
8" or 9" round cake pan. Layer with a tortilla, remaining
meat mixture, remaining tortilla, and one cup reserved
sauce. Sprinkle with ½ cup of each cheese. Bake uncovered
at 350° for 40 min.

JERRY PATE

CLAUDE PEPPER
18TH DISTRICT, FLORIDA

CHAIRMAN
COMMITTEE ON RULES

SELECT COMMITTEE ON AGING
CHAIRMAN
SUBCOMMITTEE ON HEALTH
AND LONG-TERM CARE

Congress of the United States
House of Representatives
Washington, DC 20515-0918

FRANCES H. CAMPBELL
ADMINISTRATIVE ASSISTANT
2239 RAYBURN HOUSE OFFICE BUILDING
WASHINGTON, DC 20515-0918
202-225-3931

DISTRICT OFFICE:
18TH CONGRESSIONAL DISTRICT OFFICE
300 COURT HOUSE TOWER
44 WEST FLAGLER ST.
MIAMI, FL 33130-1684
305-536-5585

MARIA TOLON
LATIN REPRESENTATIVE

LEMON CHICKEN WITH WINE

1 fryer, approximately 2½ lbs.
Garlic powder
Salt and pepper
Parsley flakes
1 sliced onion

1 sliced bell pepper
Juice from 1 lemon
½ cup of wine, your choice
Parsley flakes for topping

Cut chicken into quarters and season to taste with salt, pepper and garlic powder. Add onion and bell pepper, placing on top of each piece of chicken. Pour lemon juice and wine over entire chicken. Cover with foil and cook at 375 degrees for 1 hour. When hour is up, remove foil and brown for about 15 minutes. Sprinkle parsley on top.

Claude Pepper

Proal Perry

LOUIE'S
BACKYARD

The following recipe is excerpted from the book "A Feast of Sunlight" . . .
"The Cuisine of Norman Van Aken", <u>Random House</u> Publishers, Release May of
1988 (All Rights Reserved).

GROUPER WITH ASIAN VEGETABLES

This is a dish for its time. It is quite simple to prepare - it's
spicy and loaded with vegetables, it's good for you and I think it's
<u>delicious</u>!

FISH: 4   7-8 oz.   pieces of freshly filleted Grouper cut on a
                             severe bias

MARINADE:

1/2	Cup	Virgin Olive Oil
1	Cup	Salad Oil, such as safflower
1/2	Cup	Soy Sauce
		Juice of: 1 Orange, 1 Lemon, 1 Lime
2		Bay Leaves
6		Black Peppercorns
1	sm. bunch	Fresh Cilantro, roughly chopped
2	lg.cloves	Garlic, cut in half

Mix all of the above ingredients together in a stainless steel bowl. Make
marinade at least one hour in advance to allow flavors to blend.

GINGER-GARLIC VINAIGRETTE:

1	Cup	Red Wine Vinegar
1/2	Cup	Soy Sauce
1/2	Cup	Sesame Oil
1/2	Cup	Chopped Cilantro
1/2	Cup	Chili Oil
3	Tblsp	Peeled, Chopped Ginger
3	Tblsp	Minced Garlic
1 1/2	Tblsp	Sugar
		Freshly Cracked Black Pepper

Combine all ingredients and keep at room temperature.

ASIAN VEGETABLES: You will need approximately a 2 Cup mixture of assorted
vegetables per person   Remember, freshness is key so vary the vegetables
according to market availability -- just be sure they're in an Asian-style,
in keeping with the dish.

Suggested Vegetables:	Cucumber	Bok Choy	Purple Cabbage
	Daikon	Bean Sprouts	Yellow Peppers
	Red Peppers	Napa Cabbage	Enoki Mushrooms
	Fresh Water Chestnuts		

Cut these vegetables (substituting or omitting as necessary) on a bias as
is common with Oriental preparations. Keep cool in a bowl.

1. Prepare a hot grill (well oiled).
2. Marinate Grouper 2-4 minutes (no more or fish will taste
    overly salty from the soy sauce).
3. Grill until just done and remove to plate.
4. Remove vegetables to a slightly warm bowl, large enough to hold them
    and add the room temperature vinaigrette. (Be sure to add just
    enough of the vinaigrette to lightly coat the vegetables - you can
    reserve any leftover vinaigrette for another use). Mix in the bowl
    and then mound the vegetables over the fish. Garnish with lime and
    serve.

700 WADDELL AVENUE • KEY WEST, FLORIDA 33040 • (305) 294-1061

TROUT A' L'IMPERIALE
Four Servings

TROUT	HOLLANDAISE SAUCE
2 whole fresh trout, filleted (about 12 ounces each)	3 egg yolks
2 tablespoons unsalted butter	4 - 6 teaspoons fresh lemon juice
1 tablespoon vegetable oil	1 cup unsalted butter, melted
salt and pepper	salt and cayenne pepper
1 pound lump crabmeat, remove the cartilage and flake	

TO PREPARE THE HOLLANDAISE SAUCE:

In a double boiler, whisk the egg yolks off the heat until thick
and light in color. Whisk in four teaspoons of lemon juice and one
tablespoon of cold water. Place over simmering water, moderate heat,
whisking constantly until slightly thickened, (the egg yolks are ready
when you begin to see traces on the bottom of the pan as you whisk).
Immediately remove from the heat and gradually whisk in the melted
butter in a slow, thin stream. Season with salt and cayenne pepper to
taste. Add enough additional lemon juice to give the sauce a pleasant
tang. Keep warm over hot - not simmering - water until needed.

TO PREPARE THE TROUT:

Preheat the oven to 350 degrees. Pat the trout fillets with dry
paper towels. In a large skillet, melt the butter in the oil over
moderately high heat. Add the fillets and saute for about 30 seconds on
each side to brown lightly. Transfer to a flame-proof baking dish.
Season lightly with salt and pepper.

In a medium bowl, mix the crab with one cup of the Hollandaise
Sauce. Mound the crab mixture over the fillets, bake for 15 minutes or
until the fish is opaque throughout. At that point, increase the oven
temperature to broil. Spoon the remaining Hollandaise Sauce over the top
of the fish. Place under the broiler and cook for about thirty seconds
or until golden brown. Check frequently to prevent burning. Serve hot.

Bon Appetit
Christian Planchon

Christian Planchon
Executive Chef

Culinary Communications, Inc.

"ORIGINAL SIN" STUFFED APPLES

(serves 6)

6 medium-large baking apples
1 - 1½ cups Calvados (apple brandy)
3 Tablespoons butter
2 Tablespoons flour
2 cups light cream
2 egg yolks
Salt and pepper to taste
¼ teaspoon cinnamon
1/8 teaspoon nutmeg
1/8 teaspoon ginger
2 cups cooked duck breast, diced into small cubes
Parsley for garnish

Preheat oven to 375°

Cut tops off apples about ½" from the top. Set aside.
Core the apples a little more than you would normally,
leaving about a ¼" thick wall. Do not peel. Place the
apples and tops into a deep baking dish. Pour 1 cup of
Calvados in and around the apples. Bake in a 375°
oven for 20 - 25 minutes or until apples are almost
tender.

Melt butter in a saucepan, add flour and beat with a
whisk. Add cream and cook until just slightly thickened,
beating constantly with a whisk. Add yolks one at a time,
beating well after each addition. Add salt, pepper,
cinnamon, nutmeg and ginger and the remaining Calvados.
Blend well. Fold in diced meat.

With a spoon, remove excess liquid from inside the apples,
being careful not to break the skin. Fill each apple with
the meat sauce and replace the tops. Bake for 10 minutes
longer. Serve apples immediately on a wreath of parsley.

Marina Polvay

9315 Park Drive Suite A-1
Miami Shores, Florida 33138
Phone: (305) 758-7828 - (305) 758-8890

20 Waterside Plaza Suite 28 B
New York, New York 10010
Phone: (212) 686-2076

ST. MICHEL SALMON FILETS WITH RASPBERRY BERNAISE

4 Norwegian salmon filets (4 ounces each)
1 cup all purpose flour
3 whole eggs
½ cup half and half
1 teaspoon fresh and finely chopped basil
1 teaspoon fresh and finely chopped dill
1/3 cup white wine
1 tablespoon lime juice
Salt and pepper to taste.
1 lime, quartered
8 ounces of Brie cheese (2 ounces per filet)
Butter or margarine

Over medium heat, melt the butter or margarine in a
saute pan. Whip together the eggs and cream. Dredge
the filets in flour and then dip them in the egg
mixture, covering evenly. When the butter or margarine
begins to sizzle, place the filets, one at a time into
the pan. Shake occasionally so that butter is evenly
distributed underneath the filets. When the underside
of the fish begins to show a golden color, turn carefully
and allow the other side to cook for about 2 minutes.
Sprinkle on the fresh herbs, the white wine and then the
lime juice. Shake the pan to stir juices and transfer
the filets to a broiler pan or ovenproof serving platter.
Add salt and pepper to taste to the wine and lime juice
mixture and pour over the filets. Take the Brie cheese
and place over the filets and heat briefly under a broiler
to melt. Garnish with fresh dill and lime and serve with
raspberry bernaise on the side.

162 Alcazar·Coral Gables·Florida 33134
tel. (305) 444·1666

RASPBERRY BERNAISE
1 pkg. frozen raspberries in heavy syrup (10 ounces)
½ cup sugar
2½ cups vegetable oil
3 tablespoons crem de cassis
2 whole eggs
1 egg yolk
2 tablespoons strawberry vinegar
¼ teaspoon finely ground black pepper
1 teaspoon fresh tarragon (finely diced)

Puree raspberries with the syrup in blender. Pour puree
into sauce pan, add sugar and cassis, simmer for 30 minutes,
strain puree into a bowl through a fine sieve and allow to
cool. Place egg yolk and whole eggs into blender, blend for
30 seconds, stop the machine, add strawberry vinegar, tarragon
and black pepper. Blend until mixture is thick and pale yellow.
Blend in the raspberry puree with blender on a low speed, slowly
pour vegetable oil into the mixture and blend for an additional
30 seconds.

Note: Good shelf life and can be refrigerated.

Chef Henry Towle

Sincerely,

Alan H. Potamkin

ALAN H. POTAMKIN

POTAMKIN
21111 South Dixie Highway
Miami, Florida 33189
(305) 238-0000

123

Steaks & Seafood

CREAM OF BROCCOLI SOUP

INGREDIENTS:
2 carrots (chopped)
6 stalks of celery (chopped)
2 onions (chopped)
5 bunches broccoli (chopped)
½ cup chicken base
¼ teaspoon basil leaves
¼ teaspoon thyme leaves
1 bay leaf
1 tablespoon parsley flakes
A little white pepper and garlic salt

ROUX (THICKENER):
½ lb. butter
1 ½ cups flour
1 qt. ½ & ½ or milk

Fill 2 gallon pot half full with water and add in carrots, celery, onions, broccoli, chicken base and spices. Turn heat on. Bring to a boil. When vegetables in pot are soft, mash up with masher until there are no large chunks left.

TURN HEAT OFF!!!

Melt butter in small pot. When completely melted, mix in flour with wire whisk. Add cream (or milk) into the large pot. Mix. Add in the roux (flour and butter) in the pot. Mix in until dissolved.

Add salt and pepper to taste and a little white wine, if desired.

Mix in. Soup is ready.

Clint Ramsden

1135 N. Federal Highway/ Fort Lauderdale, FL/ (305) 561-3440

CRAB DIP - "A GREAT SOUTH FLORIDA APPETIZER"

16 oz.	Crab Meat (frozen is best)
	(you can use a <u>little</u> less crab meat)
12 oz.	Cream Cheese
1/4 cup	Mayonnaise
1/3 cup	Dry White Wine (Louis Jadot for international flavor)
	Garlic Salt to Taste
1 tsp.	Mustard
1 tsp.	Confectioner's Sugar
1/2 tsp.	Onion Juice (liquid onion)
	Dash Seasoned Salt

Soften cream cheese and blend all ingredients into cream
cheese with the exception of the crab meat. Heat in <u>double
boiler</u> and when hot and well blended, fold in crab meat.

Serves 15

Best regards,

RALPH RENICK

EGGPLANT PARMESAN

Italian breadcrumbs
½ pound ground beef
½ pound mild sausage
1 medium onion
1 green pepper
8 oz. mushrooms
16 oz. tomato sauce
16 oz. tomato puree
6 oz. tomato paste
1 lb. provolone
1 lb mozzarella
4 eggs
8 oz. oil
Italian seasonings

Soak peeled eggplant for about four hours in salt water.

Brown ground meats, onions, and pepper until tender. Add
sauces, seasonings, and mushrooms to taste.

In one bowl, beat the eggs and in another put the Italian
breadcrumbs. Dip the eggplant in the eggs, and then into
the breadcrumbs, and fry until tender.

In 9x11x2 dish, put a layer of sauce, a layer of eggplant;
another layer of sauce, and a layer of cheese. Continue
until the pan is filled. The top layer should be cheese.
Bake 30 minutes, or until the cheese is melted.

Best, Ralph

BURT REYNOLDS Jupiter Theatre

1001 E. Indiantown Road
Jupiter, Florida 33458-5191

BURT'S BEEF STEW

3 slices of bacon, cut in small pieces
4 tablesppons of flour
1 teaspoon salt
¼ teaspoon pepper
2 pounds lean beef (chuck is juicy) cut in 1" pieces
1 large onion, chopped (1 cup)
1 clove garlic, minced
1 can tomato sauce
½ can condensed beef broth
1 cup good, dry burgundy wine
1 bay leaf, if you like
1 pinch of thyme
2 carrots, cut up coarsely (1 cup)
2 stalks celery, cut up coarsely (3/4 cup)
2 potatoes, pared and cut in 4 pieces
6-8 mushrooms, sliced

Cook bacon until crisp in a large, heavy pot. Combine
flour, salt and pepper; dip beef in flour mixture to
coat completely. Brown in bacon fat, turning often.
(Add a little vegetable oil if needed.) Add onion,
garlic and brown a little. Add tomato sauce, broth,
wine, bay leaf and thyme. Cover and cook slowly for
about 1½ hours. Add carrots, celery, then potatoes
and mushrooms. Uncover and cook until meat and vegetables
are tender. Makes 4 servings.

Burt Reynolds

P A U L G. R O G E R S
815 CONNECTICUT AVENUE
WASHINGTON, D. C. 20006

ROGERS' OYSTERS

Fresh oysters on the half shell
Lemon juice
White wine
Fried bacon
Chopped onion
Ritz crackers crumbs
Butter

Serve as an hors d'oeuvres or a first course.
Select fresh oysters on the half shell -- the
number depending on how many oysters per person you
wish to serve. On each oyster, put 1/4 tsp of
lemon juice; 1/2 tsp white wine; small bits of
freshly fried bacon; about 1/4 tsp finely chopped onion;
1/2 tsp Ritz crackers crumbs and 1/4 tsp butter.

Place prepared oysters on a baking dish and
put under preheated broiler just long enough
to see that the topping is nicely brown and
beginning to bubble. Serve immediately.

MIAMI DOLPHINS

MIAMI DOLPHINS, LTD
4770 BISCAYNE BLVD., SUITE 1440
MIAMI, FLORIDA 33137
(305) 576-1000

JOSEPH ROBBIE
Managing General Partner

SHRIMP AND ARTICHOKES PIZAZZ!

This is a favorite family recipe - quick, easy, and delicious!

2 cups water
4 tablespoons butter or margarine
1 package (6¼ ounces) Uncle Ben's Fast Cooking
    Long Grain & Wild Rice
1 pound medium shrimp - cleaned and deveined
1 can (14½ ounces) artichoke hearts - drained and quartered
1/3 cup sour cream
Parsley (optional)
Lemon slices (optional)

Combine water, 2 tablespoons butter, and pkg. of rice including
seasoning packets in medium saucepan. Bring to a boil. Cover
tightly, and simmer until all water is absorbed,(approx. 5 min).
While rice is cooking, saute shrimp in skillet in remaining 2
tablespoons butter over medium heat until cooked throughout,
(2½ to 3 minutes).

Add the shrimp* and artichokes to cooked rice and stir gently.
Heat through. Stir in sour cream. Garnish with parsley and
lemon if desired. Makes 6 servings.

*If time is a problem - I buy already cooked shrimp and add to
the rice just the same.

Serve with sour dough French bread!!

Joe Rose

Joe Rose

MICKEY'S FAVORITE FRUIT SALAD

Ingredients

1 cantaloupe, cut into cubes or
scooped into balls

½ honeydew melon, prepared like
the cantelope

1 large bunch of seedless grapes
cut in half

6 ounces Gruyere cheese, diced
(you can substitute Swiss or
porvolone)

~~¼ cup salad dressing (French or~~
oil and vinegar)

½ cup shredded coconut

½ head shredded iceberg lettuce

Mix the fruit and cheese and chill
thoroughly. Toss with salad dressing
just before serving. Serve on a bed
of shredded lettuce and sprinkle with
coconut. Garnish with fresh parsley
and lemon wedges. Serve with butter
cookies if you like. Serves four.

Love and good taste!

Jan Chamberlin Rooney

Mickey Rooney

HANGMAN'S BREAKFAST

This is a favorite brunch meal.
I also enjoy it sometimes after
a late-night performance.

INGREDIENTS

3 tablespoons vegetable oil

1 medium size can of white or
  yellow hominy

2 or 3 leftover boiled potatoes

1 medium onion

1 bell pepper

1 cup leftover cooked chicken

1 large tomato

1 tablespoon chopped parsley
  (preferably fresh)

Drain the hominy and heat it in the
vegetable oil in a large frying pan.
Thinly dice the potatoes, onion, bell
pepper, chicken and unpeeled tomato
and add them to the pan. Add the
parsley. Saute until the onions just
begin to brown.

Serve with scrambled eggs and Mexican
hot sauce on the side. Makes two
portions. (If you don't have any leftover chicken, just add 4 to 6 beaten
eggs to the mixture and serve as a
main dish with hot sauce.)

131

265 NORTHEAST 26TH TERRACE
MIAMI, FLORIDA 33137

MIAMI (305) 576-5600
FT. LAUDERDALE (305) 524-5600

ELLIS RUBIN'S SUBLIMINALLY INTOXICATING LONDON BROIL

Ingredients:

     Top Round London Broil
      4 Tbsp Worcestershire Sauce
      ½ Cup Grey Poupon Mustard
        (with wine)
      2 Tbsp white wine
       Television set
        garlic powder
          salt
            pepper

Preparation At Least 2 Hours In Advance:

MARINADE AS FOLLOWS:

SPRINKLE MEAT WITH GARLIC POWDER, SALT, AND PEPPER TO
TASTE. SPREAD 3/4 MUSTARD W/SPOON OVER ENTIRE SUR-
FACE AND SIDES. THEN POUR EVENLY 2 Tbsp WORCE-
STERSHIRE SAUCE FOLLOWED BY 1 Tbsp WHITE WINE
OVER TOP AND SIDES. FLIP MEAT AND REPEAT
COVER WITH PLASTIC WRAP; REFRIGERATE.
UNGLUE YOURSELF FROM KOJAK SHOW.

Cooking Instructions:

BROIL EACH SIDE 10 - 15 MINUTES
FOR A PINK CENTER.
SLICE & DEVOUR!

Warning:

PURSUANT TO ETHICS CODE OF PROFESSIONAL RESPONSIBILITY
OF THE FLORIDA BAR, YOU AND/OR YOUR LOVED ONES
WILL NOT BE HELD IN CONTEMPT OF COOKING FOR
FOLLOWING THIS RECEIPE; HOWEVER, YOU MAY
BE SENT DIRECTLY TO JAIL IF YOU
ASK TO WITHDRAW FROM
SWALLOWING!

Yours directly from the
Ellis Rubin slammer

4431 ROCK ISLAND ROAD
FORT LAUDERDALE, FLORIDA 33319
PHONE (305) 731-4800
MIAMI 949-3101
WEST PALM 737-4996

JOHN RUFFIN, JR.
PRESIDENT, GENERAL MANAGER

JOHN AND DOROTHY RUFFIN

PEPPER STEAK

3 cups cooked rice

1 pound thin sliced
beef round

1 tablespoon paprika

2 tablespoon butter or
magarine

2 cloves garlic crushed

1½ cups beef broth

1 large onion, cut in 8ths

1 green pepper, cut in
strips

2 tablespoon cornstarch

1/4 cup water

1/4 cup soy sauce

2 ripe tomatoes, cut in 8ths

1 box frozen pea pods (optional)

Cut beef into thin strips and sprinkle with paprika; let stand
while cutting up other ingredients. Brown meat in butter. Add garlic and broth. Cover and simmer 20-30 minutes. Stir in onions and
green peppers. Cook 5 minutes more. Blend cornstarch, water and
soy sauce. Stir into meat mixture. Cook, stirring until thickened.
Add pea pods; cook 2 minutes and add tomatoes. Stir gently to heat
through. Serve over rice.

Serves: 4

Preparing: 20 minutes

Cooking: 40 minutes

DHR'S FAVORITE DELUXE CHEESE CAKE

For Crust: 2 Cups Graham Cracker Crumbs
4 Tbsp. Melted Butter
2 Tbsp. Sugar

For Pie: 2 lbs. Cream Cheese (room temperature)
2 Cups Sugar
2 Pints Sour Cream
7 Eggs
$1\frac{1}{2}$ tsp. Vanilla
$1\frac{1}{2}$ tsp. Cinnamon

Set over to 375° F.

INSTRUCTIONS

CRUST: 1. Mix graham cracker crumbs, butter, and sugar in a large springform pan
2. Press into sides and bottom
3. Refrigerate for 10 minutes

PIE: 1. Whip cream cheese until fluffy
2. Add sugar
3. Add one egg at a time
4. Whip until creamy (no lumps)
5. Fold in sour cream
6. Pour into pan
7. Bake in pre-heated oven for 50 minutes
8. Turn off oven and leave in hot oven for 1 more hour
9. Cool in springform pan overnight

Can be served topped with fresh fruit, chocolate dipped fruit, or a topping of your choice. This will serve a large party.

Mom's Macaroni & Cheese

- 7 oz pkg of Creamettes, cook about 7 minutes Drain and rinse w/ cold water

(Sauce)

- 10 oz sharp cheese (Koon brand cheese)

- 8 oz combination Jack & Swiss

- 1 cup grated parmesian

- 1¾ cup milk (whole if you want to be fat, skim if you want to be skinny)

- Dash of Worchestershire (a "dash" is of course a slightly greater quantity than a "smidge")

- 1 teaspoon of dry mustard

- Bake at 350° for 25 minutes

- Cover with swiss and/or mozzerella cheese

- Sprinkle with paprika

- Bake till a crust forms

- Serve with stewed tomatoes (serves four)

When preparing this dish please invite me over for dinner! It's my favorite.

Gerry Sandusky

Vice Rice   (Saundra Santiago)

2 cups of cooked rice
1½ cup chopped sausage
1 green pepper
1 yellow pepper
1 red pepper
1 small sweet onion
½ teaspoon cayenne pepper

Place sausage in pan and cook for 5 minutes. I recommend a
spicy sausage like Chorizo or Hot Italian sausage, but breakfast
sausage will be just as delicious.

Remove sausage from pan. Dice up peppers and onion and cook in
sausage drippings until onions become transparent. Return chopped
sausage to pan and continue to cook adding the rice. Turn gently!
Add cayenne pepper. Simmer for 1 minute and serve.

Serves 4.

A rather simple recipe that's superb as an appetizer or hor d'oeuvres. The added bonus is that it can be made ahead and freezes well in small containers. With its vervy taste, it's a wonderful prelude to dinner and does not offend a very dry white or sparkling wine.

CAPONATA ALLA SICILIANA
Eggplant Appetizer

1	large eggplant
1	teaspoon salt
1/3	cup salad or olive oil plus 3 tablespoons
2	cups onions, thinly sliced
1	cup celery, diced
2	cans tomato sauce (8 oz size)
1/4	cup red wine vinegar
2	tablespoons sugar
2	tablespoons capers
1/3	cup black pitted olives, slivered
1/2	teaspoons salt
1/4	teaspoon freshly ground pepper

Wash eggplant, cut into 1/2 inch cubes and sprinkle with 1 teaspoon of salt; let stand 10 minutes and drain. Heat 1/3 cup oil in skillet and saute eggplant until golden brown. Remove eggplant and set aside.

Heat remaining 3 tablespoons of oil (using same skillet) and saute celery and onions for approximately 5 minutes, until tender. Then, return eggplant to skillet and add tomato sauce, bringing it to a boil. Cover and cook over low heat for 15 minutes. Add vinegar, sugar, capers, olives, salt and pepper. Simmer covered and stir occasionally for 20 minutes. Chill for 6 hours or overnight.

Serves 6-8 as an appetizer

SHEILA'S PATE

1 teaspoon of rendered chicken fat (can be done
  in microwave).   Use this to grease rectangular
  cake mold, ring molds or one of your choice.

2 pounds of chicken livers, picked over and trimmed
  of all tough fibers.

3 eggs   Mix all these together
1/3 cup cognac   in a bowl.
1½ cups heavy cream

2/3 cup of diced chicken fat
1 onion coarsely chopped
1/3 cup of flour   Mix all these together
5 teasponns of salt   in a bowl.
1 teaspoon of ginger
2 teaspoons of white pepper

In three or four batches mix these two mixtures
together in a blender or cuisinart until smooth.

Pour into mold and cover tightly with double foil.
Bake at 325° for 1½ hours in larger pan filled with
hot water to just below top of mold. Cool before
unmolding.

If desired, glaze with mixture of consomme and gelatin
for smooth aspic surface.

Judy Schrafft
Mrs. George F. Schrafft

THE FLORIDA SENATE

Tallahassee, Florida 32399-1100

COMMITTEES:
Appropriations,
 Chairman
Commerce
Governmental Operations
JOINT COMMITTEE:
Legislative Auditing

SENATOR JAMES A. SCOTT
31st District

LOBSTER STUFFED TENDERLOIN

4 lb. whole beef tenderloin
2 (4 oz.) frozen lobster tails
1 tbsp. melted butter
1 ½ tsp. lemon juice
6 slices bacon, partly cooked
½ cup sliced green onions
½ cup butter or margarine
½ cup dry white wine
1/8 tsp. garlic salt

Have butcher butterfly beef. Boil lobster tails 5-6 minutes.
Carefully remove from the shells. Cut in half lengthwise and
place end to end inside beef. Combine the 1 tbsp. butter and
lemon juice and drizzle on lobster. Close meat around lobster
and tie roast securely with string at intervals of 1". Place
on rack in shallow roasting pan. Roast at 425° for 45 minutes
for rare doneness. Lay bacon slices on top and roast 5 minutes
more.

Meanwhile in saucepan, cook green onion in remaining butter
over low heat until tender, stirring frequently. Add wine and
garlic salt and heat through. To serve, slice roast and spoon
sauce over it. Delicious!

Serves 6-8

This is a special Holiday meal we have enjoyed many times.

Jim Scott

REPLY TO:
☐ 2000 E. Oakland Park Blvd., Ft. Lauderdale, Florida 33306 (305) 566-8600
☐ 346 Senate Office Building, Tallahassee, Florida 32399-1100 (904) 487-5100

JOHN W. VOGT	JOHN A. HILL	JOE BROWN	WAYNE W. TODD, JR.
President	President Pro Tempore	Secretary	Sergeant at Arms

139

NBC News　　A Division of
National Broadcasting Company, Inc.

30 Rockefeller Plaza
New York, N.Y. 10112　212-664-5488

Willard Scott
TODAY

WILLARD SCOTT'S ALL-AMERICAN COOKBOOK　Published by MacMillen

☆ Mucky Duck Homemade Key Lime Pie ☆

1 8-ounce can sweetened
  condensed milk
7 tablespoons bottled lime juice
3 large egg whites

1 prepared 9-inch graham
  cracker pie shell
Whipped cream for garnish

Mix the sweetened condensed milk with the lime juice in a large mixing bowl.

In another bowl, whip the egg whites until you find you can almost turn the bowl over without them falling out.

Add the egg whites to the bowl with the condensed milk and lime juice. Mix slowly with a whisk so as not to deflate the whipped whites. Pour the mixture into the pie shell and freeze. Serve sliced and topped with whipped cream.

Makes 6 to 8 servings.

STRAWBERRY SHORTCAKE

SIFT TOGETHER 2 CUPS OF ALL-PURPOSE FLOUR
　　　　　　　 2 ½ TEASPOONS BAKING POWDER
　　　　　　　 ½ TEASPOON SALT
　　　　　　　 1 TABLESPOON SUGAR

ADD ½ CUP OF SHORTENING (½ BUTTER AND ½ CRISCO)
ALONG WITH THAT ADD A TINY TEASPOON OF MAYONNAISE
MIX WITH FORK UNTIL MIX RESEMBLES COARSE CORN MEAL

ADD 3/4 CUP OF MILK; BLEND LIGHTLY WITH A FORK, ONLY UNTIL FLOUR
IS MOISTENED AND UNTIL DOUGH PULLS AWAY FROM THE SIDES OF THE BOWL.

TURN OUT ON LIGHTLY FLOURED BOARD AND KNEED LIGHTLY 30 SECONDS
AND ROLL WITH ROLLING PIN 3/4" THICK.

USE COOKIE CUTTER (OR JUICE GLASS WITH SMALL OPENING) TO CUT INTO
ROUNDS

PLACE ON LIGHTLY GREASED PAN

BRUSH THE TOP OF EACH BISCUIT WITH A LITTLE BUTTER

BAKE AT 475° (IT CAN BE 450-475°) for 12-15 MINUTES. KEEP AN EYE ON IT.

THEN, CUT BISCUITS IN HALF. STUFF WITH STRAWBERRIES AND WHIPPED CREAM:

 (WHIP WHIPPING CREAM. ADD SUGAR AND VANILLA TO TASTE)

TOP WITH FRESH STRAWBERRIES.

Willard Scott

E. CLAY SHAW, JR.
FIFTEENTH DISTRICT
FLORIDA

GRILLED BRISKET OF BEEF

1 Brisket of beef, any size

The night before, season with Adolph's Meat Tenderizer.
The day of cooking, season with pepper, seasoned salt,
garlic salt and garlic or garlic powder. Place on
charcoal, fat side up, for 3½ to 4 hours. Add Barbecue
Sauce and cook an additional 30-40 minutes. Let stand
or wrap in foil. Slice very thin.

BARBECUE SAUCE

1 large can of tomato juice
1 large onion chopped
2 Tablespoons vinegar
1 medium bottle Lea & Perrins Worcestershire sauce
Juice of 1 lemon
Salt, pepper and garlic to taste

Cook for 1 hour
Add 1 can of beer after 30 minutes
Add 1 can tomato puree or sauce (#2 can or 20 ounces)
     after 1 hour
Add Lowry's seasoned salt, salt and pepper to taste
Cook another 30 minutes

Enjoy!

Clay Shaw

WAXY FM V 105.9

1975 E. SUNRISE BLVD. • FT. LAUDERDALE, FL 33304 • (305) 463-9299
3000 BISCAYNE BOULEVARD • MIAMI, FLORIDA 33137 • (305) 620-9299
350 ROYAL PALM WAY • PALM BEACH, FLORIDA 33480 • (305) 659-6848

RICK SHAW'S RECIPE FOR "MRS. HUMMEL'S FETTUCINE"

INGREDIENTS:

One pound of fettucine noodles

One and one half cups of heavy whipping cream

Six to seven ounces (according to taste) of parmesan cheese

One quarter pound of butter

PREPARATION:

Melt butter on low heat   As butter melts, add cream and cheese.

Stir mixture until cheese melts. Boil noodles per package

instructions, stirring frequently.

Drain noodles well and toss with cream mix. Season with

fresh gound pepper and serve immediately.

MIAMI DOLPHINS

MIAMI DOLPHINS, LTD
4770 BISCAYNE BLVD., SUITE 1440
MIAMI, FLORIDA 33137
(305) 576-1000

JOSEPH ROBBIE
Managing General Partner

PHEASANT WITH WILD RICE

Strips of bacon to keep the pheasant moist and juicy while roasting.

1/2 c. chopped onion
4 T. butter or margarine
2/3 c. wild rice, rinsed
2 c. water
1 t. salt
6 oz. can sliced mushrooms, drained
1/2 t. ground sage
2   ready to cook pheasants 1 1/2 - 3 lbs each
6-8 slices of bacon

Cook onions in butter or margarine until tender, add wild rice, water and
salt. Cover and cook until rice is tender, 35-40 minutes. Add mushrooms
and sage. Season cavity of pheasant with a little salt; stuff with rice
mixture and tie legs to tail. Place bacon over breasts. Roast in 350 degree
oven for 1 to 2 1/2 hours, depending on size of brids. Makes 6 to 8
servings.

- By Jackie V. Shipp

GREEK CHEESE PIE - (Tyropittakia)

Ingredients:

1/2 lb   Feta Cheese

1/2 lb   Cottage Cheese

8 oz   Cream Cheese

6   Eggs

1/2 lb   Butter (melted)

1/2 lb   Filo (strudle leaves)

Filo can be bought in grocery store frozen pastry section. Mix
all cheeses together; add in well beaten eggs. Grease a 9 x 12
baking pan - Place 8 sheets of Filo (painting each sheet with
melted butter). Spoon in cheese and egg mixture; spread evenly.
Cover with 8 more sheets of Filo, same process. Fold the edges
together. Bake at 350 degrees for 45 minutes (or until golden
brown).

Joni Siani

2741 N. 29th Avenue • Suite 300 • Hollywood, Florida 33020 • Dade (305) 944-1956 • Broward (305) 925-7117 • Palm Beach (305) 655-0994

144

6 Week Bran or Blueberry Bran Muffins

15 ounce box Raisin Bran Cereal

5 cups flour

3 cups sugar

1 teaspoon salt

1 teaspoon cinnamon

Mix the above ingredients in a very large bowl.Then add the following:

1 cup vegetable oil

4 beaten eggs

1 quart buttermilk

5 teaspoons baking soda

1 tablespoon grated orange zest

Stir with a large spoon scraping up from the bottom of the bowl.Do not beat.
Spoon into a very large plastic or glass container with a tight lid,about one
gallon size.Store batter in refrigerater.Will keep perfectly for up to a 6 week
period.What a delight to have ready to bake when company drops in or for that
morning you really want a treat and don't have much time!
To bake: Spoon batter into buttered muffin cups,either 2 or 32,filling 3/4 full.
Bake in a pre-heated 350 degree oven about 18 minutes.
For another muffin delight add ½ cup either raw cranberries or blueberries
to the amount of raw batter for 2 dozen muffins,stir in gently and bake as usual.
Keep remaining batter refrigerated,and if desired place in smaller container.

Myrtle Singer

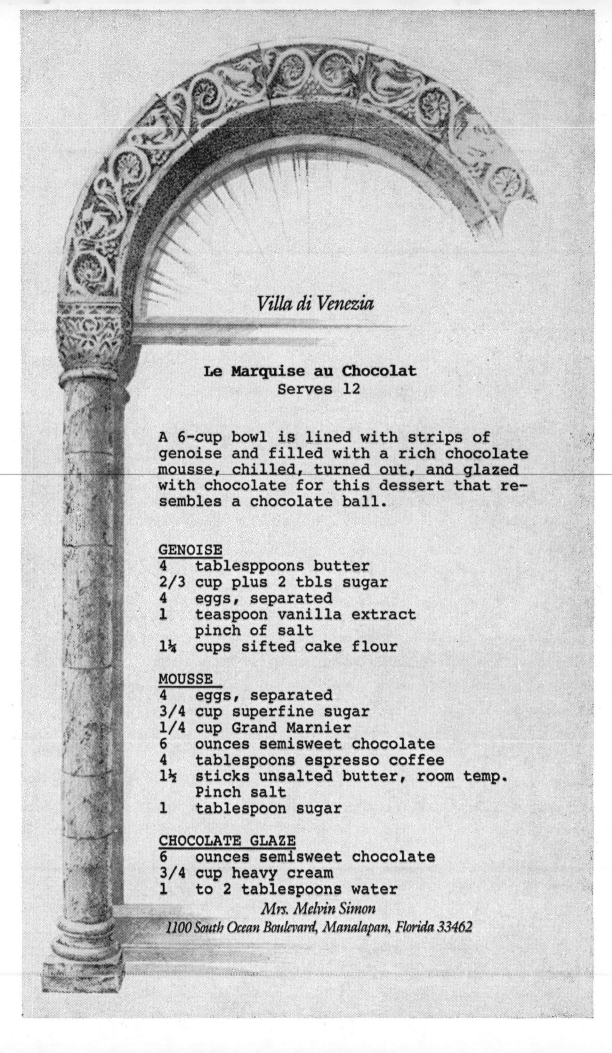

Villa di Venezia

Le Marquise au Chocolat
Serves 12

A 6-cup bowl is lined with strips of genoise and filled with a rich chocolate mousse, chilled, turned out, and glazed with chocolate for this dessert that resembles a chocolate ball.

GENOISE
4   tablesppoons butter
2/3 cup plus 2 tbls sugar
4   eggs, separated
1   teaspoon vanilla extract
     pinch of salt
1¼ cups sifted cake flour

MOUSSE
4   eggs, separated
3/4 cup superfine sugar
1/4 cup Grand Marnier
6   ounces semisweet chocolate
4   tablespoons espresso coffee
1½ sticks unsalted butter, room temp.
     Pinch salt
1   tablespoon sugar

CHOCOLATE GLAZE
6   ounces semisweet chocolate
3/4 cup heavy cream
1   to 2 tablespoons water

Mrs. Melvin Simon
1100 South Ocean Boulevard, Manalapan, Florida 33462

Villa di Venezia

GENOISE: Butter a 9-in. cake pan, lined with waxed paper, and butter and flour the paper. Melt the 4 tbls. butter and let cool. Preheat oven to 350º. Beat 2/3 cup sugar into egg yolks for 8 - 10 mins., or until thick and pale yellow. Add vanilla. Beat egg whites and salt until stiff not dry. Add remaining 2 tbls. sugar and beat until whites are glossy. Fold 1/3 egg whites into yolk mixture. Blend in 1/3 flour, then 1/3 more egg whites, then 1/3 flour. Gently fold in melted butter. Do not overmix. Keep batter light and fluffy.

Spoon into pan and bake until puffed and pulls from edges (25 - 30 mins.). Cool on rack.

MOUSSE: Beat egg yolks and superfine sugar until thick and pale yellow. Add Grand Marnier and put mixture in top of double boiler over simmering water. Beat constantly until mixture is almost too hot for your finger (4 - 5 mins.) Immediately cool over a bowl of ice, stirring until it is the consistency of thin mayonnaise.

Melt chocolate with coffee in 300º oven. Add butter bit by bit and stir until smooth and creamy. Beat chocolate mixture into the yolk mixture.

Beat egg whites and salt until stiff. Sprinkle on sugar and beat until glossy. Fold 1/3 of whites into chocolate to lighten the mixture. Gently fold in rest.

MARQUISE: Butter 6-cup stainless steel mixing bowl. Cut the genoise cake into 3 thin layers, cut 2 layers in wedges to completely line bowl. Press cake to sides. Spoon mousse in the lined bowl. Fill to top. Cover top with uncut layer of cake. Cover with plastic wrap and refrigerate, preferably overnight. Turn out into serving plate for glazing.

GLAZE: Melt chocolate in heavy saucepan with cream. Cool to lukewarm. If too oily or too thick, thin with boiling water. Spread the entire surface of the marquise with glaze, using a brush or spatula. Sprinkle with powdered sugar.

147

GENE'S CATERING

BAY SCALLOP SERVICHE   6-8 PEOPLE

```
2 LBS.    BAY SCALLOPS-MEMBRANE OR "FOOT" REMOVED
½ LB.     GREEN BELL PEPPERS-FINELY DICED
½ LB.     RED BELL PEPPER-FINELY DICED
½ LB.     ONION-FINELY DICED
2         JALAPENO PEPPERS-FINELY MINCED
6 OZ.     EXTRA VIRGIN OLIVE OIL
6 OZ.     FRESHLY SQUEEZED LEMON JUICE
1 T.      TABASCO
1/8 C. or 1 OZ. CILANTRO-MINCED
```

MARINATE SCALLOPS OVERNIGHT IN:

```
6 OZ.     FRESHLY SQUEEZED GRAPEFRUIT JUICE
6 OZ.     FRESHLY SQUEEZED ORANGE JUICE
6 OZ.     FRESHLY SQUEEZED LEMON JUICE
1 t.      CUMIN
1 t.      MINCED GARLIC
2 t.      SALT
```

NEXT DAY, DISCARD MARINADE. COMBINE SCALLOPS WITH ALL
REMAINING INGREDIENTS. TOSS. COVER AND ALLOW TO STAND
IN REFRIGERATOR 2 HOURS. SEASON TO TASTE.

        THIS RECIPE CAME TO ME FROM A PERUVIAN FRIEND & CHEF,
COMPLETE WITH ITS OWN HISTORY & ANECDOTE. I WAS AT ONCE
INTERESTED & AMUSED. ACCORDING TO THE STORY IT WAS CREATED
BY A GREAT CHEF IN LIMA WHO WON THE HEART OF HIS TRUE LOVE
WITH THE PREPARATION. ALTHOUGH THERE ARE MANY VARIATIONS,
IT IS BELIEVED THAT IT IS STILL ABLE TO SPICE UP AFFAIRS OF
THE HEART.

8944 N.W. 24 Terrace Miami, Florida 33172   Telephone: 592-1311

FLORIDA SUPERMARKETS, INC., d.b.a.

605 S.W. 16th Terrace
Pompano Beach, FL 33069 • (305) 786-3900

BAKED PINEAPPLE

Ingredients:

> 1 cup sugar
>
> 1 stick butter or margarine (softened)
>
> 4 eggs
>
> 1 can crushed pineapple, drained
>   (1 lb., 4 oz. size)
>
> 5 slices white bread, cubed

Blend together sugar, butter, eggs and pineapple. Fold in bread cubes. Bake in greased 1½ or 2 quart casserole dish at 350° for 1 hour. Serve as a dessert or a side dish with pork, chicken or ham.

Leonard E. Slider

Leonard E. Slider
President and Chief Operating Officer
Pantry Pride/Sun Supermarkets.

GRILLED QUAIL WITH KIWI COULIS

Serves 4

Ingredients	Method
4 partially boned Quail	Mix wine, vinegar, oil and seasonings. Marinate Quail in this mixture for at least 4 hours, but no more than 8 hours.
1 cup white wine	
2 Tbsp. red wine vinegar	
1 cup olive oil	
2 cloves garlic, crushed	Grill Quail over charcoal, mesquite or citrus wood fire.
1 tsp. cracked black pepper	
1 tsp. salt	
1/2 tsp. thyme	
1 bay leaf	
4 Kiwi fruit, ripe	Peel Kiwi and dice into small pieces. Mix with flavoring ingredients and heat mixture until warm. Do NOT boil or cook for any amount of time.
1 Tbsp. chopped fresh basil leaves	
2 Tbsp. white vinegar	
1/2 tsp. salt	
1/2 tsp. white pepper, ground	
	To serve, put warmed Kiwi coulis on plate. Place grilled Quail on top of coulis, garnish with fresh basil leaves and/or Kiwi coulis.

Gerald Smith
Executive Chef

On the Intracoastal Waterway at Oakland Park Boulevard
3001 East Oakland Park Boulevard,
Ft. Lauderdale, Florida 33306
(305) 561-4400

150

LAWRENCE J. SMITH
16TH DISTRICT, FLORIDA

COMMITTEE ON FOREIGN AFFAIRS

CHAIRMAN, TASK FORCE ON INTERNATIONAL
NARCOTICS CONTROL
EUROPE AND THE MIDDLE EAST
INTERNATIONAL OPERATIONS
COMMITTEE ON JUDICIARY
CRIME
MONOPOLIES AND COMMERCIAL LAW
SELECT COMMITTEE ON NARCOTICS
ABUSE AND CONTROL
DEMOCRATIC ZONE WHIP

113 CANNON BUILDING
WASHINGTON, DC 20515
(202) 225-7931

DISTRICT OFFICE:

4747 HOLLYWOOD BLVD.
HOLLYWOOD, FL 33021
(305) 987-6484 BROWARD
(305) 624-5111 DADE

Congress of the United States
House of Representatives
Washington, DC 20515

Dear Friends:

Thank you for asking me to participate in your cookbook. I would like to submit the following recipe:

MAGIC COOKIE BARS

Ingredients:

1/2 cup butter or margarine, melted (non salted)
1-1/2 cups graham cracker crumbs
1 cup chopped walnuts and pecans (mixed)
1 cup (6-oz. package) semi-sweet chocolate pieces
1-1/2 cups (3-1/2 oz. can) flaked coconut
1 can Eagle Brand sweetened condensed milk

Procedure:

Pour melted butter onto the bottom of a 13 x 9 x 2 inch pan.
Sprinkle crumbs evenly over melted butter
and pack down like a crust.
Sprinkle nuts evenly over crumbs.
Scatter chocolate pieces over nuts.
Sprinkle coconut evenly over chocolate pieces.
Pour sweetened condensed milk over coconut (evenly).
Bake in moderate (350 degrees) oven, 25 minutes or until
lightly browned on top.
Cool in pan 15 minutes.
Cut into bars.

LAWRENCE J. SMITH
Member of Congress

LJS:eh

151

Here's a recipe for preparing what are often called garbage fish, because for one reason or another nobody likes to eat them. In this case, it's for chain pickerel which certainly doesn't have the aura of largemouth bass or even the utilitarianism of bream.

Make a marinade using wine vinegar, pickling spices, 2 bay leaves, oregano, and virgin olive oil.

Clean the fish, gut it, remove the head.

Place it in an aluminum baking dish (9 x 13 recommended), cover with the marinade, and place in refrigerator for 24 hours.

Remove pan from refrigerator, throw away the marinade and the fish ... and eat the pan.

(Recommended beverage: six pack of any cheap beer.

My Mother's Spaghetti Sauce (This is for real!)

1 onion chopped fine
1 stalk celery chopped fine
2 cloves garlic chopped fine
¼ lb. sweet sausage
1 lb. ground chuck
1 large can (28 oz) tomatoes
1 12 oz can tomato paste
5 bay leaves
1½ tbsp. worcestershire sauce
pinch fennel
1 cup red wine

Saute onion, celery and garlic.
Brown meat, drain excess fat.
Add tomatoes and paste; simmer.
Add bay leaves, fennel and worcestershire, and cook for 2-4 hours over low heat.
Add water as needed for preferred consistency.

Thom Smith

Aunt Anne's Strudel

½ lb. butter - room temperature
1 cup sour crean
2 cups unsifted flour
Pinch of salt
1 tablespoon of sugar

Mix together in a bowl by hand. Chill in refrigerator
overnight. Cut dough into 4 pieces. Flour a board
and roll out thin.

Cover dough with melted butter, sprinkle with cinnamon
and sugar mixed together, spread apricot and peach
jam over dough, sprinkle with chopped walnuts, coconuts
and raisins. Roll up like a jelly roll and put on
greased cookie sheet (with sides). Brush top with
butter. Cut half way through ⟨/ / / / /⟩ and
bake at 350° for 50-60 minutes. (preheated).

Remove from oven and finish cutting through each.
Sprinkle with powdered sugar and cool on a rack.

Howard Socol
Chairman of the Board
Burdines

Summers
P. O. Box 16
Sagg Main Street
Sagaponack,
New York
11962

Telephone
516-537-3006

Winters
9210
Blind Pass Road
Siesta Key
Sarasota, Florida
34242

Telephone
813-349-1282

Syd Solomon

Weary from four grim years in the Army in WW II, I came to
Florida to pursue my career as an artist. It was tough to
make a living while trying to catch up on painting.
I discovered that there were wonderful fish to be caught in
Sarasota's bays and gulf. I learned all about Florida fishing
methods, and about the variety of fish being caught, particularly
about the great game fish, SNOOK. Now, rightfully, this great
fighter is protected by all of us who yearn for its survival.
However, if you are lucky enough to catch a legal snook, you
might try an old easy-to-do recipe for what we use to call
              " Snook In Tin"
(The title began because we called aluminum foil, Tin-Foil then)

Using an 18" square of heavy-duty foil coated on one
side with either cooking oil or butter, place slices
of lemon, and onion rings on the botton. Place a fillet
of the fish on top, and cover it with the following sauce;
        Make a roux using two tablespoons of flour
        and two tablespoons of butter. When lightly
        browned add some capers and a tin of anchovies
        and crushed garlic, cook until anchovies are
        well intergrated, add dry white wine and minced
        dill.
Cover the fillet with the sauce. Slice a hard-boiled
egg on top, and wrap the foil tightly around all. Place
over hot coal, in an oven until fish is cooked.
Serve with yellow rice, and a good bottle of wine.

SUNBEAM TELEVISION CORPORATION

Bob Soper, Meteorologist

BUTTER RUM BANANAS

6 bananas
½ cup brown sugar
3 Tbsp. lime juice

1 tsp. allspice
¼ cup rum (Myers's is best)
¼-½ cup butter

Mix all ingredients except bananas in a large frying pan
over low heat until well-blended and the brown sugar melts.
Add the bananas that have been peeled and halved lengthwise,
as well as crosswise. Cook slowly, turning often until the
bananas are well coated and soft. Serve with a scoop of
vanilla ice cream.

Bob Soper

WSVN / NBC   1401 79th Street Causeway, Miami, Florida 33141 (305) 751-6692

PaesanoRestaurants

We are pleased to share our typically Italian pasta recipe with our friends. This is one of our personal favorites.

LINGUINI and BROCCOLI AGLIO OLIO

Ingredients

    1 bunch fresh broccoli
    2 tbs. salt
    1 lb. linguini
    3/4 cup olive oil
    8 cloves garlic, peeled and chopped
    Pinch red pepper
    Parmesan cheese

Preparation

Remove tough bottom stems from broccoli. Cook for 10 minutes or until tender in boiling water. Drain broccoli and save water. Bring 4 quarts of water to a boil in 6-qt. pot. Add the reserved broccoli water. Add salt and bring back to a boil. Add linguini. Cook for approximately 12 minutes. Drain (cooking time varies with different brands of pasta--taste-test).

Heat the oil and saute garlic and red pepper until garlic is soft. Add the broccoli and linguini. Toss together.

Serving

Serve with grated cheese on top. (4 servings)

Boun Appetito!

Mario Spinaci

Maria Spinaci

1301 East Las Olas Boulevard • Fort Lauderdale, Florida 33301 • Phone 467-3266
3850 North Federal Highway • Lighthouse Point, Florida 33064 • Phone 942-0006

156

Nancy Stafford

KEY LIME CAKE

As a sixth generation Floridian it distresses me to know that
<u>real</u> Key limes are becoming extinct. Bottled Key lime juice,
available at your grocery market, may be successfully used
if necessary.

        1 box Duncan Hines Lemon Supreme
            cake mix
        1 3-1/2 ounce package instant lemon
            pudding mix
        4 eggs
        1/2 cup water
        1/2 cup key lime juice
        1/2 cup vegetable oil

Beat all ingredients at high speed for 2 minutes. Pour into
fluted tube pan or 9-by-13-inch pan. Bake in preheated,
350° oven for 35 to 45 minutes. When cool, frost with glaze
made by mixing 2 cups confectioners' sugar and 1/3 cup lime
juice.

This is tart and fresh tasting.

Good treat while you watch "MATLOCK"!!

Best wishes -
Nancy Stafford

M.Sterling

218 S.W. 1st Avenue
Fort Lauderdale, FL 33301
305 / 467-7321

Claudia's Lasagna
(Serves 12)

1/4 c. olive oil	Heat oil. Add onions, finely chopped,
2 med. onions	minced garlic and stir until golden.
4 med. clove garlic	Add meat. Brown.
4 lb. lean gound beef	Add spices.
1 T. oreg.	Add tomato paste and sauce and wine.
3 tsp. salt	Turn heat to low.
1 tsp. pepper	Cook 1 1/2 hr. Stir occasionally.
2 6oz. can tomato paste	
2 8oz. can tomato sauce	Boil salted water.
1 c. dry red wine	Cook noodles 20 min.
1 lb. lasagne noodles	Drain & dry noodles.
2 1/2 lb. ricotta	
1 lb. mozzarella	Grease 2 11" X 7" pyrex dishes.
12 heaping T. grated Parmesan	Cover with noodles, sauce, then ricotta,
	On top of each pan of lasagna put half
	mozzarella, sliced thin and half of the
	Parmesan cheese.

Preheat oven to 350.° Bake 45 min. - 1 hr.

158

STOLLE'S SPECIAL BARBEQUE MARINADE

```
2    TBSP SUGAR
2    TBSP SALT
1/2  TBSP CINNAMON
2    TBSP SOY SAUCE
2    TBSP WORCESTERSHIRE SAUCE
1/2  CUP SHERRY OR WINE
```

COMBINE THE ABOVE INGREDIENTS, MAKING SURE TO MIX WELL. POUR MARINADE MIXTURE OVER LONDON BROIL OR YOUR FAVORITE TYPE OF STEAK. COVER AND REFRIGERATE FOR 24 HOURS, TURNING MEAT 2 TO 3 TIMES.

City of Miami, Florida

XAVIER L. SUAREZ
MAYOR

P. O. BOX 330708
MIAMI, FLORIDA 33233-0708
305-579-6010

Black Bean Soup

Ingredients: 1 lb. black beans, 10 cups of water; 2/3 cups of olive oil; 1 large onion, 4 cloves of garlic, one bell pepper, 4 teaspoons of salt, 2 teaspoons of oregano, 1/3 cup of vinegar.

Directions: Wash beans and soak in water. When beans are swollen, bring to boil until soft (approximately 45 minutes). In a separate pan, heat oil and saute onion and garlic and pepper all chopped up. Put approximately a cup of beans in pan and mash them. Pour everything in pan into boiling pot, add salt and oregano. Let boil approximately one more hour then add vinegar. Simmer for one more hour so it thickens.

Flan

Ingredients: 9 eggs (3 whole, 6 yolks), 1 cup of milk, 1 can of evaporated milk (12 ozs.), 1 can condensed milk (14 ozs.), 1/4 teaspoon salt, 1/4 teaspoon vanilla extract.

Sauce: 1/4 cup of sugar.

Directions: Beat egg combination well, add milks, salt and vanilla, set aside. For sauce, use pan which can be placed in pressure cooker. Melt sugar until caramelized, coat as much of pan as possible with sauce, pour egg and milk mixture into coated pan, cover tightly. Place pan in pressure cooker with 1/4" of water, close pressure cooker. After steam comes out, cook 5 minutes, remove from burner and let sit for 15-20 minutes. Take covered sauce pan from pressure cooker and refrigerate for 2 hours (minimum). To serve, uncover, place a plate on top of pan and invert pan. Then carefully lift off sauce pan.

FLORIDA POWER & LIGHT COMPANY

<u>MYSTERY COOKIES</u>

```
2 Cups Brown Sugar      )
1 Cup Flour             )    Mix together
2 Tsp Baking Powder     )

1 1/3 sticks melted or very soft butter
Pinch of Salt
2 well-beaten eggs

Lastly:  1 Tsp Vanilla
         1 Cup Chopped Pecans
```

Mix all of the above ingredients in
large bowl.

Pour into a 9 x 12 pan that has been
lined with wax paper. Bake at 325
degrees for 45 minutes.

While hot, turn out of wax paper and cut
into 2" x 2" squares. Cool slightly.
Shape by rolling into oblong pieces and
then rolling twice in sifted powdered
sugar.

George Sullivan

MICHAEL TALBOTT

<u>Watermelon Chicken</u>

4 chicken breasts
2 cups of watermelon juice (fresh)
1 tablespoon of cooking oil
ginger

Brown chicken breasts in oil for approximately 4 minutes. Remove from pan. Mix ginger (to taste) with watermelon juice, (any fruit juice can be substituted). Pour into pan and mix with droppings.

Place chicken back into pan and cook for 5 minutes. Remove and serve over rice.

Serves 4.

MIAMI, FLORIDA

FLORIDA SEAFOOD LINGUINE

COOKING TIME: 3 1/2 - 4 HOURS. SERVES 4 HEARTILY.
UTENSILS NEEDED:
8 QT. STOCK POT, 10 - 12 QT. SPAGHETTI POT, LADLE, WOODEN SPOON.

INGREDIENTS:

1/4 cup OLIVE OIL	1 tbs CHEF PAUL PRUDHOMMES "SEAFOOD MAJIC"	1 doz CHERRYSTONE CLAMS
1 medium size ONION (mince)	SAFFRON (.2 grams)	1 lb SEA SCALLOPS
6 cloves GARLIC (crush)	1-28 oz can PROGRESSO PEELED TOMATOES	1 lb large SHRIMP (peel & devein)
1 tbs BASIL	2-28 oz cans PROGRESSO CRUSHED TOMATOES w/puree	4 FLORIDA LOBSTER TAILS (shell, devein, & cut)
PARSLEY SPRIGS (as garnish)	DRY WHITE WINE	1 lb DOLPHIN FILLET (cut into pieces)
2 BAY LEAVES	2-1 lb boxes LINGUINE	

EXTRAS:

CHAMPAGNE, SALAD OF YOUR CHOICE, FRENCH BREAD

STEP BY STEP PREPARATION AND COOKING:

1) SCRUB THE CLAMS IN COLD WATER, DRY AND REFRIGERATE.
2) PREPARE THE REST OF THE SEAFOOD INTO SHRIMP SIZE PIECES, COMBINE IN A BOWL, COVER AND REFRIGERATE.
3) USING THE 8 QT. STOCK POT OVER MEDIUM HIGH HEAT, SAUTE THE ONION, GARLIC, BASIL AND "SEAFOOD MAJIC" IN THE OLIVE OIL.
4) OPEN THE PEELED TOMATOES AND USING YOUR HANDS SQUASH THE TOMATOES TO BITS ONE AT A TIME INTO THE POT. STIR AND LET COOK WHILE YOU OPEN THE CRUSHED TOMATOES.
5) ADD THE JUICE LEFT FROM THE PEELED TOMATOES, BOTH CANS OF THE CRUSHED TOMATOES AND A CAN OF 1/2 WATER AND 1/2 DRY WHITE WINE, USING AN EMPTY TOMATO CAN AS THE MEASURE.
6) BRING THIS MIXTURE TO A BOIL, ADD THE BAY LEAVES AND REDUCE HEAT TO LOW. COOK UNCOVERED, STIRRING EVERY 15 MINUTES FOR 3 TO 3 1/2 HOURS UNTIL THICK.
   * DURING THIS TIME, YOU CAN CHILL THE CHAMPAGNE, MAKE THE SALAD AND SET THE TABLE.
7) ADD THE CLAMS, SHELL AND ALL, TO THE SAUCE. RAISE THE HEAT TO MEDIUM AND COVER.
8) IN THE 10-12 QT. POT, BOIL WATER AND ADD 1 1/2 TBS. SALT AND 2 TBS. OLIVE OIL.
9) STIR IN THE SAFFRON AND THE PREPARED SEAFOOD TO THE SAUCE AND LEAVE UNCOVERED.
10) PLACE THE LINGUINE IN THE BOILING WATER AND COOK FOR 8-10 MINUTES ALTERNATELY STIRRING THE SAUCE AND THE LINGUINE EVERY MINUTE.
11) DRAIN LINGUINE WHEN DONE AND KEEP CHECKING AND STIRRING SAUCE.
    * WHEN THE CLAMS HAVE ALL OPENED, THE SAUCE IS DONE.

TO SERVE:

PLACE A BED OF LINGUINE ON EACH PLATE. PLACE 4 CLAMS AROUND THE EDGES AND THEN LADLE THE SEAFOOD SAUCE OVER THE LINGUINE. GARNISH WITH PARSLEY SPRIGS AND HEATED SLICES OF FRENCH BREAD.

ENJOY!

GEORGE TERRY
TERRYTUNES INC.
HOLLYWOOD, FLORIDA

163

LA FERME RESTAURANT
1601 E. SUNRISE BOULEVARD
FT. LAUDERDALE, FLORIDA, 33304
764-0987

LES CRÊPES PARMENTIER

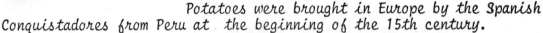

Potatoes were brought in Europe by the Spanish Conquistadores from Peru at the beginning of the 15th century.

France was the last European country to accept them. At the end of the 17th century Antoine Augustin PARMENTIER, in one of his many attempts to introduce them to the French people, planted a field of potatoes outside Paris. He installed guards to make it attractive, with the order that they should close their eyes on the thieves.

Well, the potatoes were stolen and since have become an every day food and countless recipes have blossomed all over the country. From the rustic potatoes au "Gratin" to the spectacular potatoes "Soufflées".

The most delicate of all and which are very famous in my part of France, North East of LYON are:

LES CRÊPES PARMENTIER (Potatoes Crêpes)

Serves 6

INGREDIENTS:

1 lb. of peeled potatoes
1/2 cup of milk
3 table spoons of flour
5 eggs
4 table spoons of heavy cream
8 ounces of clarified butter.

METHOD:

Cook the potatoes in salted water, make a purée. Let it cool for 10 minutes. Stir with a wooden spoon or in the kitchen aid mixer. Then add the milk, the eggs (one at a time), the cream and finally the clarified butter.

Use a large frying-pan, heated and oiled ligthly with a full brush. Drop slowly a spoonfull of potatoes mixture, (it will spread by itself), and turn over to cook each side. You can make 4 to 6 crêpes in the pan depending on its size.

SUGGESTIONS:

LES CRÊPES PARMENTIER can be used as garnish to a meat dish in sauce and also as a DESSERT, spreading confectionned brown sugar and dipped in raspberry coulis.

HENRI TERRIER   Owner Chef

MARIE-PAULE TERRIER Hostess

164

S P A G H E T T I   C A R B O N A R A

NOT SERVED AT THE MAI-KAI, BUT ONE OF OUR FAVORITE "AT HOME" RECIPES.

1 LB. - SERVES 4 TO 6 PEOPLE

SAUCE:

10 EGGS - BEAT IN LARGE BOWL
3/4 LB. FRESHLY GRATED ITALIAN PARMESAN CHEESE

Mix together 'till sauce gets thick and gloppy.

ADD:

4 TSP. FRESHLY CHOPPED PARSLEY
1 TSP. FRESHLY GROUND PEPPER
2 TSP. ITALIAN SEASONING
1 TSP. OREGANO
1 TSP. WORCHESTERSHIRE
½ TSP. LAWRY'S SEASONED SALT

Put bowl in oven to warm for 10 minutes at 150°.
Check & stir - do <u>not</u> let it cook eggs.

BACON MIXTURE:

1 LB. LEAN BACON - SLICE INTO 3/8" PIECES

Put in frying pan - cook 'til brown - medium heat

ADD:

½ RED ONION (QUARTERED)
2 TSP. ITALIAN SEASONING
1 TSP. OREGANO
1 TSP. SAMBAL OLEK OR OTHER HOT, SPICEY RED PEPPER ITEM

After bacon mixture is brown & pretty well done, but
not crisp, add

2 OZ. LIEBFRAUMILCH OR OTHER DRY WHITE WINE OR CHAMPAGNE
1 OZ. DRY VERMOUTH

Saute for 2 - 3 minutes over high heat.

SPAGHETTI:

1 LB. THIN SPAGHETTI - COOK W/SALT 8-10 MINUTES

Let bacon cool a little, then mix with warm bowl of egg
and cheese (include bacon grease and wine) and mix.

Blanche spaghetti in colander w/hot water, Put spaghetti
in large warm platter, pour sauce over and mix with wooden
fork and spoon. Dish up on hot plates & eat immediately.

Serve with a fine red wine.

ROBERT F. THORNTON

the polynesian restaurant / 3599 north federal highway / fort lauderdale, florida 33308 / telephone 563-3272

Thank you for including me in the Celebrity Cookbook.
I hope you know I don't do fancy dishes. I'vd never
had time to be more than a short-order cook; so what
I eat is usually quick and simple.

Herewith the promised recipe for EASY CHEESEY SOUFFLE:

Heat, but do not boil, 1 cup milk and
3 tbs. butter.

In a blender, put
1 thin slice white bread
½ tsp dry mustard
½ tsp salt
Pinch nutmeg

Cover and blend on high speed 5 seconds.

Then gradually add:
The hot-milk mixture
1 cup diced Cheddar cheese,
firmly packed

Blend 10 seconds.

Add 4 egg yolks and blend 12 seconds more.

In a 1½ quart souffle dish, beat 4 egg whites
until stiff but not dry.

Gradually pour cheese mixture over egg whites,
folding in with a rubber spatula until lightly
blended.

Bake in a 375 degree oven for 35 minutes.
Serves four.

This is a good luncheon dish, served with fresh asparagus,
sliced tomatoes drizzled with Italian dressing and hot rolls.
Sherbet for dessert.

Bon apetit!

Molly Turner

WPLG/TV 10 BROADCAST HOUSE   3900 BISCAYNE BOULEVARD   MIAMI FLORIDA 33137 • (305) 576-1010
BROWARD NEWS BUREAU 1 FINANCIAL PLAZA   FT. LAUDERDALE FLORIDA 33301 • (305) 763-4577

I R I S H   B R O W N   B R E A D

1	cup unsifted all-purpose flour
2	tablespoons sugar
1	teaspoon baking powder
1	teaspoon baking soda
½	teaspoon salt
1½	tablespoons butter or margarine
2	cups whole-wheat flour (stone-ground if possible)
¼	cup rolled oats
1½	cups buttermilk
½	cup Miller's Bran

Combine all-purpose flour, sugar, baking power, soda, and salt.
Cut in butter until in very small particles. Stir in whole-wheat
flour, the Miller's Bran and rolled oats well. Make well in
center; add buttermilk. Stir lightly but throughly until all
flour is moistened. Turn out onto lightly floured board; knead
5 times. Gather into ball; place on lightly greased cooke sheet.
Pat into 7-inch circle. Using sharp knife, make large cross on
top of loaf to allow for expansion. Bake at 375°F 40 minutes,
until loaf is browned and sounds hollow when tapped. Remove
from oven; place on rack. Brush with melted butter. Allow to
cool before serving. Makes 1 loaf, 7 inches in diameter.

Monsignor Bryan O. Walsh

ACCREDITED

Member: National Conference of Catholic Charities
Child Welfare League of America
An Equal Opportunity Employer
A Loving service of the Archdiocese of Miami Ministry of Christian Service

167

CAROL A. WEBER
Associate Publisher

This is one of my favorite foods. I have eaten it in German
restuarants in many parts of the United States and in Germany
near my husband's home town, but I have never found it any better
than what I cook at home using an old recipe given to me by my
Scotch/Irish mother.

SAUERBRATEN

3 lbs. beef	1 tsp. peppercorns
3 slices salt pork (cut thin)	12 cloves
salt & pepper to taste	1/4 cup sugar
2 cups water	1 tbsp. fat
2 cups vinegar or white wine	6 gingersnaps
2 medium sized onions	1/4 cup flour
3 medium sized bay leaves	1 cup sour cream

Use bottom round cut of beef, chuck or Boston cut. Cut slits in
beef and insert thin slices of salt pork. Rub with salt and
pepper. Place beef in large bowl. Heat vinegar or wine and
water, pour over meat. Add sliced onions, bay leaves,
peppercorns, cloves and sugar. Cover bowl and refrigerate.

Let stand for 48-72 hours, turning meat each day.

Remove meat, discard pork strips, and wipe roast dry. Heat fat
and brown meat on all sides. Strain and add 2 cups of marinating
liquid and gingersnaps. Cover pot. Cook on medium heat until
tender.

Place meat on platter. Add flour and sour cream to liquid. Stir
until thickened. Strain and serve.

Guten Appetit!

Carol Weber

BEEF ROULADEN

4 ROULADEN (THINLY SLICED TOP ROUND STEAK CUT TO
          APPROXIMATELY 6" X 12")
SALT
PEPPER
HOT GERMAN MUSTARD
BACON
STEAK TARTAR
ONIONS
DILL PICKLES

Place Rouladen, flat, on a large platter. Sprinkle
with salt and pepper. Then brush lightly with hot
mustard. Cover with diced onions, small uncooked
bacon pieces and crumble Steak Tartar over Rouladen
surface. Place a 1/4 pickle width-wise in middle.
Roll up and secure with round tooth picks or very thin
metal skewers. Place Rouladen in large frying pan and
brown in margarine on high heat. When brown, pour 1/4
cup water in frying pan, cover and let simmer until
water has evaporated and Rouladen have browned
further. Add 1 cup water and let simmer 30 minutes.
Take Rouladen out and thicken gravy to desired
consistency. Then return Rouladen to gravy for 2-3
minutes.

Serve Rouladen with boiled potatoes or dumplings and
red cabbage.

This dish always brings back fond memories of Sunday
Family Dinners. ENJOY,

Gerald Weber
President/CEO

SPIRITS, INC.
110 EAST BROWARD BOULEVARD
SUITE 2050
FORT LAUDERDALE, FLORIDA 33301

THE FLORIDA SENATE

Tallahassee, Florida 32399-1100

SENATOR ELEANOR WEINSTOCK
26th District

COMMITTEES:
Agriculture
Executive Business
Natural Resources and Conservation

CHOCOLATE PIE

Serves 6-8

In a double boiler, melt:

    1   6 oz. package of semi-sweet chocolate bits

    18 marshmallows, regular size

    1/8 cup of milk

When dissolved, add:

    1/2 tsp. vanilla

    1 packet Knox Gelatin (1 Tbsp.)
    dissolved in 1/8 cup of milk

Cool, then combine with:

    1/2 pint of heavy cream, whipped

Fill baked graham cracker crust with above mixture. Cover
with sweetened whipped cream when ready to serve.

REPLY TO:
☐ 319 Clematis Street, Suite 617, West Palm Beach, Florida 33401 (305) 832-5122
☐ 328 Senate Office Building, Tallahassee, Florida 32399-1100 (904) 487-5356

170

HUMMING BIRD CAKE

9" - 3-layer cake

[3 cups   all-purpose flour
[2 cups   sugar
[1 teaspoon   baking soda
[1 teaspoon   salt
[1 teaspoon   ground cinnamon

3 eggs, beaten
1 cup vegetable oil

1½ teaspoon vanilla extract
1- 8 oz. can crushed pineapple,
                undrained
1 cup chopped pecans
2 cups chopped bananas

Cream Cheese Frosting
1/2 cup chopped pecans

Combine first 5 ingredients into a large mixing bowl. Add eggs
and oil, stirring until dry ingredients are moistened. DO NOT BEAT.
Stir in vanilla, pineapple, 1 cup pecans and bananas.

Spoon batter into 3 greased and floured 9" round cake pans.
Bake at 350° for 25-30 minutes until wooden toothpick inserted
in center comes out clean.

Cool in pans 10 minutes; remove from pans and cool completely.

Spread frosting between layers and on top of cake and also on
sides of cake. Sprinkle 1/2 cup chopped pecans on top.

Yield - one 3-layer cake (9")

Cream Cheese Frosting

1- 8 oz. pkge. cream cheese, softened
1/2 cup butter or margarine, softened
1- 16 oz.package powdered sugar, sifted
1 teaspoon vanilla extract

Combine cream cheese and butter, beating until smooth. Add
powdered sugar and vanilla. Beat until light and fluffy.
Yield enough for 9" 3-layer cake.

ANGIE and GENE WHIDDON

DENISE'S BROCCOLI CASSEROLE
in MUSHROOM SAUCE with CHICKEN

2 SERVINGS

4 SKINNED CHICKEN BREASTS
1 CAN OF CREAM OF CHICKEN OR CREAM OF CELERY SOUP
1 CUP OF MAYONNAISE
1 TEASPOON OF CURRY POWDER
  PEPPER
  MILK
  CELERY
  ONION
1 TEASPOON OF LEMON JUICE
  BREAD CRUMBS
  GRATED CHEDDAR CHEESE

BOIL CHICKEN BREASTS WITH ONION, CELERY AND LEMON JUICE
UNTIL THEY'RE TENDER.
STEAM BROCCOLI.
TO MAKE MUSHROOM SAUCE POUR SOUP INTO A SAUCEPAN. USE
MILK INSTEAD OF WATER. ADD 1 CUP OF MAYONNAISE AND 1
TEASPOON OF CURRY POWDER. ADD PEPPER TO TASTE. STIR AND COOK.
CUT UP THE CHICKEN AND PLACE IN THE BOTTOM OF A
GREASED CASSEROLE DISH. LAYER WITH BROCCOLI AND MORE CHICKEN.
POUR ON SAUCE. SPRINKLE GRATED CHEDDAR CHEESE ON TOP. ADD LAYER
OF BREAD CRUMBS. BAKE AT 350 FOR ABOUT 20 MINUTES. ENJOY.

Denise White

WSVN / NBC   1401 79th Street Causeway, Miami, Florida 33141 (305) 751-6692

Clement C. Winke Jr.
President and Publisher

The Best Baked Beans

1   15 oz. can B&M baked beans, drained

1   cup diced onion

3/4 cup diced green pepper

4-5 slices of bacon cut in 1" pieces

Mix above ingredients together and add sauce.

Sauce:

3/4 cup maple syrup

2   tbls. brown sugar

1/2 cup catsup

1   tsp. prepared mustard

Add sauce to above mixture and combine
thoroughly. Bake, uncovered, 45 minutes
to 1 hour.

Clement C. Winke Jr.

33 SE 3rd Street / Boca Raton / Florida 33432 / 305-395-8300
307 NE 2nd Avenue / Delray Beach / Florida 33444 / 305-278-1200

KNIGHT-RIDDER NEWSPAPERS

the fisherman

GROUPER FISHERMAN

6 - 8 - 10 oz. Fresh Grouper Fillets
2# Fresh mushrooms sliced
6 oz. Toasted sliced almonds
1 Pint garlic sauce (recipe follows)
5 oz. White wine
4 oz. Flour
6 oz. Melted butter

Procedure

Place a large sautee pan on high heat
Add the butter
Dredge fish in flour then put into hot fat
Brown on one side turn over and add all the wine
Place in a hot 450° oven
Cook till it flakes when pushed with a fork. Place on plate
Saute the mushrooms in butter
Season with salt & pepper
Place a suitable amount on top of each fillet
Top each fillet with 2 oz. of garlic, sauce and a sprinkle of toasted almonds

GARLIC SHERRY SAUCE

4 Cloves garlic chopped fine
2 Shallots chopped fine
4 oz. Dry Sherry
1 Pint heavy cream
5 oz. softened butter
Salt & Pepper

Sautee the garlic and shallots in a sauce pan over low heat
Cook till soft
Add the Sherry and heavy cream and bring to a boil
Remove from heat
Using a whisk in the butter in 4 stages
Adjust seasoning with salt & pepper

BON APPÉTIT

Rudy Wojo

3880 North Federal Highway, Fort Lauderdale, Florida 33308

ADIROLF ENTERPRISES, INC.
P. O. BOX 24344
FORT LAUDERDALE, FLORIDA 33307

WOODY WOODBURY

CHILI DRUMSTICK STEW

Slice	4	Carrots into 1-inch sections
Slice	2	White onions (thick slice)
Slice	3	Celery stalks into 1- inch sections
	3	Cloves
	4	Jalapeno peppers
	3	Bay leaves
	1	(Approx. 12-oz can processed Okra)
	3	"squirts" Tabasco sauce
	6 to 8 oz.	Cooking wine (or regular Port wine)
	1 cup	regular white flour.

Gently stir and mix all of above into crock pot.

Cook on "LOW" setting for 8 hours.

At end of 8 hours, place 6 thoroughly cleaned
and washed chicken drumsticks into crock pot
along with 1 can (12 oz.) processed chili
con carne.

Gently mix and stir these two additional
ingredients down into the heart of the stew.

Cook another 2 to 2½ hours on "LOW" setting.

Serve with garlic bread (toast) and any large
iced beverage, such as tea, coffee, lemonade,
beer, or highball. Chilled white wine com-
plements this treat most of all.

It's terrific!

P.S. Just before serving, re-stir and mix
gently and thoroughly.

175

Aunt Ginny's B/B Pickles

4 (Large Onions
25 (Cucumbers —soak overnite in
ice — Slice thinly cukes & onions,
layer upon layer, in large Kettle
Cover with ½ C Salt —let stand 1 hr
Drain-carefully!
   Bring to boil: 1 Qt. Vinegar, 2 C Sugar
   2 T each (White Mustard Seed,
            (Celery Seed
            (Gr. Ginger
   1 ✕ . tumeric

Add to pickles + cook only
until a boil begins— stir often
use large spoon + turn over
& over — change of cdor will occur.
Do not overcook or they will
loose crispness — Place in clean,
sterile pickle jars! Yummy!!!

Virginia S. Young

Virginia S. Young
(farmer Mazur)

RECIPE INDEX

South Florida's CELEBRITY CHEFS

Sponsored by
THE MONTEREY VINEYARD

Proceeds to benefit the
MUSEUM OF ART
Fort Lauderdale

Compiled by the Contemporaries

Foreward by DON SHULA

If you would like to support the Museum of Art by ordering additional copies, send:

$9.95 per copy plus $1.50 for postage and handling fee (2 or more books, $2.50 postage and handling). Washington State residents must add 7.9% sales tax.

Please send me ___ copies

BILL TO:

Name _____

Address _____

City _____ State ____ Zip _____

SHIP TO:

Name _____

Address _____

City _____ State ____ Zip _____

☐ Payment enclosed   ☐ Charge

Visa # _____ Exp. Date _____

MasterCard # _____ Exp. Date _____

Signature _____

PEANUT BUTTER PUBLISHING

329 - 2nd Avenue W. ▪ Seattle, WA 98119 ▪ (206) 281-5965
1- 800 - 426 - 5537